DA 3122 74809
6.50

D0553835

THE CHURCHILL TANK

A Churchill VII with 75mm gun (see page 61).

THE
CHURCHILL
TANK

The story of Britain's most famous tank, 1939–1965

by

PETER CHAMBERLAIN and CHRIS ELLIS

ARMS AND ARMOUR PRESS

4

Published by
Arms and Armour Press
677 Finchley Road
Childs Hill
London NW2

First Published 1971
ⓒPeter Chamberlain and Chris Ellis, 1971
ⓒLionel Leventhal Limited, 1971
All rights reserved

SBN 85368 042 6

Printed and bound in Great Britain

Contents

List of Abbreviations

Certain standard abbreviations are used throughout this book. For the benefit of readers unfamiliar with them, these are as follows:

AA anti-aircraft
ARV armoured recovery vehicle
AVRE armoured vehicle, Royal Engineers
BARV beach armoured recovery vehicle
CDL canal defence light
MG machine gun
Mk Mark
pdr pounder (gun calibre)
RE Royal Engineers
REME Royal Electrical and Mechanical Engineers

Introduction

MOST famous of all British tanks, the Churchill was also in service for longer than any other, nearly 25 years, although this record seems likely to be eclipsed in due course by the Centurion. Named after Britain's wartime Prime Minister, the Churchill was, if for no other reason, better known to the public at large than any other British tank. It was designed to a conception — the slow moving infantry support tank — which was quickly proved outmoded by Germany's effective, swift, blitzkrieg armoured tactics even before the first Churchill tank was built. In true British military tradition, the Churchill was, in fact, conceived in 1939 to exploit the conditions of the previous war of 1914-18, the trench warfare stalemate which the first British tanks were so successful in breaking. In the event, therefore, the Churchill provided a unique evolutionary link between the lozenge-shaped tanks of 1918 and the fast, low, heavily gunned vehicles which had emerged by 1945.

This book covers the whole story of the Churchill tank from the first designs of 1940 until it was 'retired' from the British Army (though not from some other armies) in 1965. In the intervening years it had come to close demise early on but, somewhat outmoded and outgunned as a fighting tank, had proved enormously successful due to its inherent toughness, size, and steadiness, as a basis for the ingenious range of 'funnies' or 'tin openers' evolved for the invasion of Europe in 1944. Special purpose versions of the Churchill were among the first Allied tanks to land at Normandy to punch the holes in the West Wall for the following gun tanks. The full range of all these 'funnies' is described and illustrated here — the AVREs, Goats, Bobbins, Crocodiles, Onions, Snakes, Congers, and scores of other weirdly-named and weird-looking developments seemingly inspired by Heath Robinson but, in reality, tough and (mostly) lethal and effective instruments of war.

The basis of this book is a series of articles first published in Airfix Magazine in 1967-68. However, the entire story has now been re-written in much greater detail and is very much expanded as a result, with a good deal of additonal information not previously published. In more than 120 photographs it has been possible to illustrate almost every variant of the Churchill ever produced and many of these pictures have never before appeared in print. It must be pointed out that the quality of a few of these photographs is poor but this, we feel, is more than compensated for by their rarity value.

In preparing this book we must acknowledge the help of Mr. D.Mayne, Mr G.Pavey, and Mr E.Hine of the Imperial War Museum Photographic Library for help in locating pictures, and Mr D.Nash of the Imperial War Museum Reference Library. John Milsom, R.Surlemont, Richard J.Hunnicutt and Col. R.J.Icks, USAR(Retd), have also assisted in locating details, etc, of us various individual types described. The illustrations are reproduced by courtesy of the Imperial War Museum, Hilary Doyle, Col. R.J.Icks, Chris Ellis and John Milsom.

Due to the very large number of pictures involved, this volume has a separate pictorial section which is virtually a book in itself telling the story of the Churchill tank in pictures. The text is cross-referenced, where appropriate, to illustrations in the pictorial section for the added guidance of readers. All facts and figures, except where needed to embellish the story, are confined to the appendices in Part 3.

A Russian Churchill IV, knocked out on the Eastern Front. This was one of a quantity of Churchills of various marks supplied to Russia under Lease-Lend.

1.
Gestation and Birth

The A20

The Churchill's origin dates back to September 1939 when the General Staff drew up requirements for an infantry tank design to be known as the A20. This had to be even more heavily armoured than the then new A12 Matilda infantry tank. With memories of the static trench warfare conditions of World War I still dogging the War Office, a good trench-crossing ability was considered particularly necessary. Vickers were the first firm to be consulted on the A20 project, in late September 1939, when they were asked for an opinion on its feasibility.

Described in the General Staff specification as a 'shelled area' tank, the A20 was envisaged as something like the Mk VIII tank of 1918, able to cross 'no man's land', immune to shell fire and capable of taking on the heavy defences of the Siegfried Line. It was to be capable of surmounting 5ft obstacles in forward gear and 4½ft obstacles in reverse with a gradient ability of 30°. Armour thickness was to be 80mm, ground pressure was to be as low as possible, and top speed was to be 10mph. No track covers were to be fitted, so enabling an 'unditching' beam to be used as in the 1918 tanks. For similar reasons the track was to be of the all-round type with the armament in side sponsons and a central command position on the hull top.

The Mechanisation Board, who decided design policy, soon amended this original specification. At a meeting on 25 September 1939, they decided that armour thickness of 60mm would be sufficient to withstand the German 37mm anti-tank gun and that a fully traversing turret would be much superior to sponsons. This would enable the weight to be kept to 32tons and to facilitate rail transport. It was proposed to use an existing engine and transmission in the design to cut out development time and Dr. Merritt, the Chief Superintendent of Tank Design, had earmarked the Meadows DAV Flat-12 engine and Wilson epicyclic gearbox from the A13 Mk III cruiser tank which was then in the development stage.

Outline design proceeded at the Tank Design Department, Woolwich, and on 28 October 1939 Harland and Wolff were asked to undertake detailed design in conjunction with the Department, followed by production of 50 or 100 vehicles.

Choice of the Belfast firm was largely dictated by the fact that at the time it had a large and unused productive capacity when engineering firms elsewhere were already engaged on other war work. Initially Harlands were told that their 300hp diesel engine might be used as an alternative to the Meadows unit, but this proposal fell through at an early stage, in January 1940, owing to lack of development. So that progress with the design could be reviewed, no definite contract for production was confirmed until 9 February, when four pilot models and 100 production vehicles were ordered.

Meanwhile, consideration was given to the armament. The General Staff wanted a larger gun than the 2pdr, and the 6pdr, then in the design stage, seemed ideal. However, provisional dimensions showed that the muzzle would project two feet ahead of the A20's front horns, which was thought undesirable. In any case considerable development was still needed on the 6pdr which could not be ready until 1941. The 3in and 3.7in howitzers were briefly considered, but the first could only fire smoke shells at that time (no HE ammunition being available), and both suffered from low velocity. The 2pdr therefore seemed the only possible weapon and on 12 January it was decided to mount this weapon in the turret, with a short calibre naval 6pdr (similar to those used in World War I tanks) mounted between the front horns. This latter idea was soon dropped, however, when the Ordnance Board pointed out that the low muzzle velocity of a short 6pdr would give indifferent performance. As an alternative the new French 75mm tank gun was suggested for the hull, but as this would have added about two tons to overall weight and necessitated considerable design changes the Department of Tank Design rejected the idea.

The weight limit remained a problem and as finalised it was decided to fit A12 (Matilda) turrets to the first two pilot models, A20E1 and A20E2, with the 2pdr gun and co-axial .303in machine gun as in the A12. A 2pdr gun, 2in smoke mortar, and .303in MG were to be carried in the hull front with a further .303in MG recessed into a small sponson in each side of the hull (plate 1). The second two pilot models, A20E3 and A20E4, were to have specially designed turrets with electric traverse and provision for the possibility of mounting the new 6pdr gun.

By 11 June 1940 the first pilot model, A20E1, made in mild steel was ready for its first run, though at this time it lacked its turret and armament. The A20 was 27ft 1½in long, 9ft 9¾in high, and 9ft 2½in wide, with 14 small independently sprung bogie wheels each side and 'overall' tracks. The finalised design weight had increased from the 32tons first requested to 37½tons on paper. The A20E1 greatly exceeded this, however, scaling 43tons. The preliminary run was brought to a premature halt after four miles when the gearbox seized up. Sufficient data was taken, however, to show that armament would have to be reduced to a single 2pdr gun only in order to cut the overall weight since the vehicle was severely underpowered. The alternative was to fit a more powerful engine and, in fact, Vauxhall Motors Ltd of Luton were at this time working on just such a unit specifically for the A20, to replace the Meadows engine. Known as the Bedford Twin-Six, the Vauxhall engine was basically two 6cyl commercial truck engines coupled together in Flat-12 configuration. Vauxhall had become involved with the A20 programme on 12 February 1940, soon after the first production order had gone to Harland and Wolff. To expand production facilities still more, Vauxhall were asked to participate with the A20, for which purpose the Ministry of Supply would build and equip a new factory at Luton. Vauxhall would run the factory and also develop and build their own engine for the tanks they produced.

From A20 to A22

As the A20 was in so many ways unsatisfactory, it was decided to terminate the entire project late in June 1940 when only the A20E1 and A20E2 had been completed. Apart from the poor performance another prohibitive factor of the A20 was its excessive weight which no military bridging equipment in service in 1940 could support. Even before the formal cancellation, a revised, lighter (under 40 ton) design for the Infantry Tank Mk IV was considered necessary, retaining all the characteristics of the A20 but with superior performance. A preliminary specification was drawn up early in June by the Department of Tank Design under the designation A22, and Vauxhall were asked to carry out detailed design utilising their new 350hp Twin-Six engine as the power plant. This engine was by now running, having been produced in the short time of three months following the original plans to produce the A20. Meanwhile, to save time and assist in working out the new design, the A20 drawings and the A20E1 pilot model, now with a simulated wooden turret (plate 2), were sent to Vauxhall at the end of June.

It should be remembered that at this period demand for tanks was at a premium, most to the BEF's armoured equipment having been lost in the fighting in France. At this time, in fact, Britain had less than 100 tanks of all kinds left to face the German panzer divisions if the expected invasion (Operation Sea Lion) took place. The new Prime Minister, Winston Churchill, took characteristically vigorous steps to redress the balance and on 29 May 1940, at the time of the Dunkirk evacuation, he ordered the setting up of a Tank Board charged with investigating the best ways of improving tank procurement and design. Churchill met the Tank Board on 11 June 1940, and it was decided that 500 to 600 models of the proposed new infantry tank would be required by March 1941. The pilot model was to be ready for trials by November 1940 and production was to start the following month. By the time of Churchill's next meeting with the Tank Board, on 20 July 1940, they had approved the outline specification for the revised design, and top priority was given to getting the vehicle into production with 'utmost rapidity' and 'utmost enthusiasm', as Churchill put it.

Detailed design of the A22 was started at once and 12 draughtsmen were loaned to Vauxhall from the Mechanisation Board Design Section to carry out this work. The new vehicle was now fully designated A22 Infantry Tank Mk IV. A mock-up of the A22 was viewed by the Tank Board in November 1940, a little behind the optimistic schedule, but only just.

The first pilot model of the A22 was undergoing tests by December 12, 1940 (plate 3) and the first production models, in mild steel, were completed in March 1941 (plates 4, 5). Both King George VI and Prime Minister Churchill were early visitors to the Vauxhall factory to see the new tank for themselves. By this time the practice of naming tanks had been adopted for ease of identity, and from June 1941 A22 was called the Churchill, much to the Prime Minister's delight and very appropriately in view of his keen interest in its development.

Delivery of the first 14 completed production models was made to the Army on 30 June 1941, a big shortfall on the initial over-optimistic schedule but nonetheless a remarkable achievement even by urgent wartime standards — from drawing board to production in less than a year. Vauxhall had no previous experience of tank production though they had had earlier military contracts for their Bedford trucks.

The Early Churchill

The hull of the Churchill was constructed on a graduated armour basis of 3½in front, 3in side, and 2½in rear thickness. In general the method of construction was to attach the armour plate to an inner skin of ½in mild steel riveted to mild steel angles at the joints, special bolts being used to secure the armour plate to the skin. The turret was cast on a 3½in basis and carried a crew of three, consisting of commander, gunner and loader, the rest of the crew being made up of driver and front gunner in the hull. The floor of the hull was flat and free from projections and was divided into four compartments. At the front was the driving compartment, which also housed the front gunner; immediately behind was the fighting compartment containing the electrically-traversed three-man turret. Behind this again was the engine compartment containing the Bedford 350bhp Flat Twin-Six engine, and behind the engine compartment was a transmission compartment housing the gearbox, steering brakes and main brakes, the air compressor and power traverse generator.

The power plant had been designed to be as compact as possible while the radiators and petrol tanks were placed alongside the engine and were protected by heavy armour plating against splash. Transmission featured the Merritt-Brown four-speed gearbox, which provided controlled differential steering. The Churchill was the first production vehicle to use this. (More details of this gearbox appear in Appendix 1.)

Panniers were provided at each side of the hull between the upper and lower runs of the track, these being used for storage of equipment. The tank was carried on 22 bogies, each independently sprung, 11 each side, and the tracks were of the steel articulated link type being spudded or webbed. Flanged steel wheels on the bogies carried the vehicle on the double rail section of the track links. Double doors were provided in the roof above the driver and front gunner as escape hatches and a square door was also fitted into each side of the hull, opening into the driving compartment. Periscopes were provided in the hull roof for the driver and gunner and were also fitted in the front of the turret. Armament consisted of a 2pdr QFSA gun and 7.92mm Besa machine gun co-axially mounted in the turret with a 3in QFSA howitzer in the front hull plate. A 2in smoke mortar was mounted in the turret-roof.

This then was the Infantry Tank Mk IV, Churchill I, a 38.5ton vehicle with 100mm frontal armour, a speed of 17mph and a cruising range of 90 miles, the first of a series that ran to eight basic models that varied in gun-power, armour and so on. Reworked models (modifications and the addition of appliqué armour) brought the series ultimately to total 15 marks.

2.
The Production Models

When Churchill production began in the middle of 1941, the need was for tanks in quantity, and to achieve maximum output Vauxhall Motors acted as design and production 'parents' for a group of contractors who were to build this vehicle for either the full or part duration of the war. In addition to Vauxhall, Broom and Wade, Birmingham Railway Carriage, Metro-Cammell, Charles Roberts, Newton Chambers, Gloucester Railway Carriage and Wagon, Leyland Motors, Dennis Bros, Harland and Wolff, and Beyer Peacock all built Churchills, and dozens of light engineering firms made components; at the peak of production more than 600 firms were involved. As these firms got into their stride, with Leyland and Metro-Cammell building their first Churchills in June and July 1941 respectively, production quickly built up; by October 1941 no less than 400 vehicles had been completed by the member firms of the production group.

From the beginning a number of design faults revealed themselves. In particular the clutch gave trouble and many other components had a tendency to wear out after only a short life. Some vehicles had to be returned for mechanical overhaul after failing their military acceptance tests after 150 miles (or less) of running. Such problems were almost inevitable, however, in a 'drawing board' design of this sort, for many components or sub-assemblies were put into production after bench-testing only. The urgency was such that there was just no time for the extended running trials and service tests usual in the days of peace.

By November 1941, however, it was clear that these early short cuts were rebounding on the entire programme. In a War Office report that month it was stated that all Churchill tanks so far delivered were unfit to be sent overseas (to the Middle East) or even used on active service in Britain unless 16 major modifications were made. Ten of these involved the transmission and steering, three the suspension, and three the hull. There were five other modifications requested which were desirable but less urgent. These major modifications broke down into no less than 158 detail changes which included the incorporation of added armour protection for the hull.

The 're-work' programme

While major faults were remedied on the production line and design changes were incorporated in new vehicles as soon as practicable, it was not possible to incorporate modifications in the earlier vehicles until sufficient Churchills had been produced to allow their temporary withdrawal from service. As a temporary measure Vauxhall attached an engineer to tank brigades armed with Churchills and a check was kept on all faults and maintenance problems arising in service. By May 1942 production reached 191 new vehicles per month and the first of the older Churchills were withdrawn for 're-working'. Of the first 1,200 Churchills built, no less than 1,000 had to be re-worked to overcome the

initial design faults and it was not until early 1943 that the War Office reported 'substantial progress ..... in eliminating defects'.

In addition to mechanical improvements, other changes included the adoption of track covers — made in three pieces to simplify removal for maintenance — the addition of appliqué armour to the vertical front plate and sides, the addition of stiffeners in the front horns, and the fitting of new side air intakes which had the louvres on top instead of in the sides. This latter allowed the fitting of trunking for wading and obviated the tendency to take in water when fording shallow streams.

The major design change was the removal of the 3in howitzer from the hull front. By virtue of its position it was limited in traverse and field of fire, and the stowage space for the 58 rounds of 3in ammunition carried in the vehicle could be utilised more usefully. A 7.92mm Besa machine gun was therefore installed in place of the 3in weapon, and the vehicles so fitted were designated Churchill Mk II (plates 8, 9). Some Churchill IIs were built as such while others were re-work conversions from Mk Is. An interesting variation, built in small numbers, was the Churchill IICS (plate 11) a close support version which simply changed over the gun disposition of the Mk I so that the 3in howitzer was carried in the turret and the 2pdr in the hull.

The 6pdr Arrives

The service career of the Churchill reflected closely the 1940-45 period. Several times it came close to being phased out of production, only to be reinstated, modified, or re-armed, following the fortunes of war and consequent reformulation of requirements.

The first major change in the Churchill's production history came with the introduction of the 6pdr gun in place of the 2pdr. This arose from a War Office decision in June 1940 to develop and fit a gun of this calibre to all tanks, to match the 50mm weapon which the Germans were then known to be developing. Hesitation and delay in these early days, however, were to cost Britain dear in the crucial years ahead. The 6pdr as a replacement for the 2pdr had been mooted as early as April 1938 when its specification was discussed at the War Office and the Director of Artillery was asked to draw up a detailed design. However, as his design department was already fully stretched on other work and there was no indication of priority from the War Office, nothing further was done. A year later, in June 1939, the War Office took the matter up again, and this time work was started on producing a prototype. This was completed and tested in Spring 1940 and on 10 June 1940 the Ministry of Supply, responsible for tank production, asked for 400 6pdrs as quickly as possible for mounting in tanks. Though the War Office themselves now wanted the 6pdr to replace the 2pdr (in view of the impending German 50mm gun) they would not sanction 6pdr gun production at that time lest it disrupt 2pdr output. This attitude persisted until February 1941, but meanwhile the Ministry of Supply had contrived to increase their

Left: Prime Minister Winston Churchill boards the first production Churchill tank in June 1941.

initial order of 14 pilot model guns to 50 in October 1940 and, two months later increased this to 500 in order to get a production line going. In February 1941 the War Office relaxed their original inflexible attitude and 7,000 6pdrs were ordered; the following May, when Rommel's panzers were first encountered in Libya, this order was doubled. These guns were to be produced for tanks and anti-tank field carriages in the ratio 6:4. Thus the 6pdr entered production, but a vital year had been lost in getting it into service.

In the meantime work started on adapting existing tank designs to take the 6pdr gun. In the case of the Churchill, still then known only as the Infantry Tank Mk IV, the go-ahead was given in April 1941. A completely new and larger turret was needed since the original turret was not big enough to accommodate the 6pdr. The Tank Design Department worked out the new turret and designed and tested three different types — welded, cast, and bolted. A major problem was finding a firm to produce the new turret, but in August 1941, after firing trials were completed, the welded turret was judged the best and a production order was placed for this type with Babcock and Wilcox. Presumably because Vauxhall were considered busy enough sorting out the Churchill's teething troubles, there was a remarkable lack of liaison between the Department of Tank Design and Vauxhall over the matter of the new turret. The result was that when Vauxhall finally received design details in October 1941 they found it to have several impractical features which would need changing for mass production by member firms of the Churchill group. Vauxhall therefore did a very quick redesign job on the turret which was finally ready for production by Christmas 1941.

With the 6pdr gun and new turret, the Churchill Mk III was born (plates 13, 15 and 16). The prototype was completed and passed its final inspection on 9 February 1942. The earliest Mk IIIs had the early type of air intakes and uncovered tracks as in the Churchill II, but from about March-April 1942 all new Mk IIIs appeared with covered tracks, new air intakes with top instead of side openings, and the other changes resulting from the re-work programme. Similarly re-worked Mk Is and IIs were returned to service so altered even though they retained their original turrets and 2pdr guns. By 10 July 1942, the Churchill III was being built at the rate of 40 a week and about this time Vauxhall and Broom and Wade had started converting old Mk I and IIs to Mk IIIs at the rate of 15 — later 25 — a week by substituting the new turret and re-working them in the usual way to latest production standards. The appliqué armour added during re-working was, incidentally, indirectly linked to. the adoption of the 6pdr gun. When the War Office first refused to sanction 6pdr gun production they suggested instead that the Churchill could meet the threat of the German 50mm tank gun more adequately by having its armour maximum increased from 3in to 3½in.

Concurrent with the Churchill III, another version of the vehicle was being built with the same 6pdr main armament, but differing considerably in external appearance by having a cast turret. This was the Mk IV (plate 17) which was produced by Metro-Cammell, Charles Roberts, Leyland and Beyer Peacock. Specification of the Churchill III and IV was essentially the same but the cast turret of the Mk IV offered slightly better armoured protection than the welded turret of the Mk III. The turret was based on the cast prototype designed and tested by the Department of Tank Design but owing to limited casting facilities it supplemented rather than replaced the welded turret used in the Mk III.

In the Mk III and IV form the Churchill had already increased considerably in weight and hitting power compared to the Mks I and II. Brief characteristics of the 6pdr-armed Churchills were as follows:
Weight 82,908lb; length 24ft 1.3/8in; width overall 10ft 8in; width over tracks 9ft 2in; ground contact 12ft 6in; track width 22in; fuel 150gallons plus 32½ gallons in an external fuel tank; road range 127miles; cross-country range 60miles; power/weight ratio 8.45hp/ton; power 325bhp at 2,200rpm; turret ring diameter 54½in; main armament 20°elevation, 12½°depression; armour – hull front 101mm glacis plate 38mm/70°, nose 88mm, side 76mm, rear 50mm, floor 19mm, hull top 15-19mm, turret front and side 89mm, turret 76mm, turret roof 19mm (Mk III) or 35mm (Mk IV). In addition most vehicles had 20mm of appliqué armour on the hull sides. The gun was either the 6pdr OQF Mk 3 or 5, the latter being distinguished by its noticeably longer barrel with added counterweight.

With increasing numbers of Churchill Mks III and IV available, the Mks I and II rapidly disappeared from first-line use from the end of 1942 onwards. Many of these early marks were, in any case, converted to Mk IIIs, or special purpose variants. Others were relegated to training units. A few Churchill IIs (and IIIs) were sent to Russia together with Valentines and Matildas in 1942, but do not appear to have been rated very highly by the Red Army. By Soviet standards these vehicles were under-gunned and later in the war they were relegated to acting as escort tanks for the SU-152 assault guns. Some Mk Is remained in service longer, however, using their 3in howitzers to provide the close support needs of Churchill regiments operating outside Europe. They were used in small numbers in Tunis and Italy, in the latter theatre often with another 3in howitzer replacing the 2pdr gun in the turret.

In a typical month, January 1943, production of the Churchill reached 160 new vehicles with another 100 vehicles re-worked to Mk III standards from earlier marks.

Blooded in Action

Churchill tanks were first used in action during the raid on Dieppe, on 19 August 1942. This was the first landing over an enemy-held beach on any large scale in the European conflict and many lessons were learned for the future, particularly in the deployment of armour in amphibious operations. The Churchills taking part were mainly Mk IIIs with a smaller number of Mk Is, and the 14th (Canadian) Calgary Tank Regiment was the unit involved (plate 18). Thirty vehicles were sent across the Channel in LCTs but only 28 actually landed. All were waterproofed for deep wading with trunking and exhaust stacks, and leading vehicles carried a primitive form of bobbin to lay a chestnut paling over the shingle and so make a trackway for the following tanks. Three of the Churchills had been fitted with experimental flame-throwing equipment, these being known as Okes (plates 20 and 21). All three were knocked out before they could be used against the enemy.

Of the gun tanks which landed, many were knocked out before they could clear the beaches and only a few vehicles managed to surmount the sea wall and engage the enemy. As a result of this action the Germans were able to acquire and evaluate the Churchill at an early stage in its life (plate 21). Dieppe taught that specialised armoured vehicles would be required for future landings and such types as the AVRE, the BARV, and the carpet layers stemmed directly from the experiences of the Canadian Churchills in this brave but abortive action.

Churchills played only a minor part in the Western Desert fighting of 1942. Two Mk IIs had been sent to Egypt for desert trials as early as December 1941, but these were inconclusive due to the poor condition of the vehicles on arrival. Three Churchill IIIs were later sent to Egypt and these were allocated to 1st Armoured Division for trials. They were present at the Battle of Alamein in October 1942 but in an insignificant role as Brigade HQ vehicles. One was knocked out by a German 88mm gun and the other two became unserviceable. However, the propaganda value of Churchills in the desert was tremendous and their presence was well publicised with numerous dramatic photographs (plates 23, 24, 25) though there was no indication at the time that only three vehicles were involved. The fact was, however, that by War Office thinking at that period, the Churchill was unsuitable for desert warfare. It was too slow. Experience in the Western Desert campaigns of 1941-42 against Rommel's fast tanks suggested that speed and reliability were more important than heavy armour protection in tank actions, at least in the open conditions of the desert. Priority was now given to 'heavy cruiser' tank development, principally the A27 Centaur/Cromwell designs and it was decided to cease Churchill production when existing orders were completed (which would have been about the end of May 1943). Vauxhall and the other firms in the Churchill production group would then switch to building Cromwells.

However, events took a turn in the Churchill's favour when the chance came to prove it in battle. The Churchill III (together with the Churchill IV) went into large-scale action with the First Army in Tunisia, in the hands of the 25th Tank Brigade, and later the 21st, in January 1943 (plate 26). In the close hilly country of Tunisia enemy anti-tank guns and tanks once again had the advantage of concealment and open warfare of the desert where speed was a major advantage became a thing of the past. In Tunis, the Churchill vindicated itself as a vehicle capable of taking punishment and proved most successful in its designed role as an infantry support tank. Appearance of the early German Tiger tanks clinched its reprieve and plans were put in hand to provide the Churchill was a heavier armament for the battles that lay ahead.

The 75mm gun

In the Western Desert fighting of 1942 the balance had swung in Britain's favour as far as tanks were concerned when the American-built Grant and Sherman entered service and demonstrated decisively the value of the 75mm gun with its ability to fire HE as well as AP rounds and so give indirect fire support. The British 2pdr and 6pdr guns fired only AP shot which meant that artillery support had to be called in (if available) to engage 'soft' but vital targets like emplaced anti-tank guns. Though a small proportion of CS (close support) versions of British tanks, were available armed with howitzers, their main task was firing smoke and, in any case, they were not provided in sufficient numbers to give adequate HE support fire for the other tanks.

Experience with the Grant and Sherman, coupled with vociferous requests from tankmen themselves led to a War Office decision to adopt a 75mm weapon for British tanks and in January 1943 plans were made to fit this to the Churchill Since 75mm gun production would be limited at first, however, and was also needed for other tanks, it was decided to aim for a strength of approximately 30 per cent of Churchills armed with the 75mm weapon. Another 10 per cent would be armed with 95mm howitzers for the close-support role only, and the balance would continue to mount 6pdrs. A further expedient at this period — and purely a local one — was the fitting of the complete 75mm M3 mounting and mantlet taken from discarded Sherman tanks to standard Churchill IVs. This was done by 21st Tank Brigade Workshops in Tunisia and 120 vehicles were so modified. The resulting conversion was known as the Churchill IV(NA 75)–NA meaning North Africa — and these vehicles were used with great success in the subsequent Italian campaign. The Churchill IV (NA 75) carried 75 rounds of 75mm shells, The NA 75 conversion remained in service (in Italy) until the war's end (plate 27).

The British version of the 75mm gun was developed by Vickers and was basically a bored out 6pdr which fitted the 6pdr mount. Work on this weapon started in December 1942. Though the first guns of this type were ready at the end of 1943, it was February 1944 before teething troubles with this weapon were ironed out. The British 75mm gun could fire American ammunition.

A small number of Mk IIIs were converted to carry 75mm guns, but the first 'standardised' production Churchill to carry the British made 75mm gun was the Mk VI which, apart from the armament, was identical to the cast-turret Mk IV. It carried 84 rounds of 75mm ammunition (plates 35 and 36). The Churchill V was, in the meantime, a version of the Mk IV fitted with a howitzer for the support role, firing HE only as a replacement for the Mk I which had remained until then (1943) the only version of the Churchill with howitzer armament. The conversion was carried out by the Royal Ordnance Factories. It was identical to the Mk IV except for its armament which was the QF 95mm tank howitzer Mk I with a co-axial 7.92mm machine gun; 47 rounds of howitzer ammunition were carried (plate 31).

Peak year for Churchill production was 1943 and 18 per cent of all British tanks built that year were Churchills — only the Valentine and Crusader were built in larger numbers. The Germans were now using the Tiger and late-model Pz IVs in Italy, and the Churchill with 75mm gun in that closely-confined country was proving its worth with its heavy armour, if only because nothing with a bigger punch and better protection was available.

Major redesign

In an attempt to improve on the basic Churchill, the opportunity was taken with the 75mm gun requirement to incorporate all the lessons learnt in action with earlier marks in an entirely new model. The Churchill VII, designated A22F (plates 32, 33, 34) was virtually a complete re-design of the Mk VI though externally the appearance remained very similar. The fundamental change was a new hull which incorporated in a single thickness — of up to 6 in — the basic hull and the appliqué armour of the older marks. This altered the overall dimensions by an inch or two. The square side escape hatches gave place to circular hatches intended to reduce the armour weakness in this position, and the driver's vision hatch in the vertical front plate was replaced with a circular hatch. The turret was also a complete re-design, having cast sides and a welded roof. Improved vision was provided for the commander by the installation of a raised vision-block cupola in place of the previous rotating hatch. The weight was increased by these improvements to 40 tons, and the top speed reduced to 13 mph. Main armament was a QF 75mm gun Mk 5 or 5A with 84 rounds of ammunition, and there were two Besa machine guns − one co-axial − with a total of 6,525 rounds of ammunition. Precise armour thicknesses were as follows: hull front 152mm, glacis plate 57mm/70°, nose 140mm, sides 95mm, lower side 57mm, rear 50mm roof 16-19mm, floor 19-25mm, turret front 152mm, turret sides 94mm, turret roof 20mm. The Churchill VII entered production at the end of 1943, and was the principal British heavy tank to take part in the invasion of NW Europe in June 1944, and in the subsequent 1944-45 campaigns. It formed the main equipment of the 31st and 34th Tank Brigades and the 6th (Guards) Tank Brigade. The earlier Mk VI with 75mm gun was also, of course, used operationally at this time. The final main production version of the Churchill as a combat tank was the Mk VIII which was in all respects identical to the Mk VII, except that it was armed with a 95mm howitzer as fitted in the Mk V (plate 39).

With the introduction of the Mk VII in November 1943, work was started to convert Mks III, IV, V, VI, to Mk VII status. Most of this conversion work was carried out by the REME workshops. Retrospective fittings included later model 6pdr guns or 75mm guns, Mk VII type vision cupolas and sights, and of course, added armour. New Mark numbers were allotted as follows:

Churchill Mk IX: Mks III and IV with heavier composite cast/welded Mk VII type turret, reinforced roof and re-armoured with appliqué armour consisting of thicker front plates, and the addition of skirting plates to the hull. Ordnance QF 6pdr Mk 3 or 5 fitted.

Churchill Mk IX LT: As for Mk IX, but retaining the original turret unaltered. 'LT' stands for 'Light Turret'.

Churchill Mk X: Mk VI reworked with heavier composite turret, reinforced roof and re-armoured with appliqué side armour. New visor and glacis plate, heavy suspension units and H41 gearbox as in the Mk VII were other changes. Ordnance QF 75mm gun Mk 5 or 5A was fitted in this mark.

Churchill Mk X LT: as for Mk X, but retaining original turret (plates 37 and 38).

Churchill Mk XI: Mk V reworked incorporating a heavier composite turret, appliqué side armour, thicker front plates reinforced roof and the addition of skirting plates to the hull. Ordnance QF 95mm Tank Howitzer Mk I remained the main armament on this model. This was essentially the Mk V brought up to the Mk VIII standard.

To enable the heavier turret on the Mks IX, X, XI, to be traversed, a special turret traversing gear was fitted to replace the original type.

From early 1945 onwards numbers of these Churchills reworked to the latest standards appeared. Relatively few, however, had the heavy turret fitted and most were of the LT type. These could usually be distinguished from the original marks by the vision cupola and, in most cases by the extra appliqué armour, though this was not always so obvious, and varied in style.

3.
The AVRE

Though the Dieppe raid had been unsuccessful, it led to the development of many of the specialised types of armour (the so-called 'funnies') used in the invasion of Europe in 1944. One particular item of equipment shown to be wanted was some form of protection for the assault engineers who had sustained heavy casualties under fire while trying to breach the sea wall and other obstacles on the Dieppe beaches. In August 1942 when the lessons of Dieppe were being evaluated, Lieutenant J. H. Donovan of the Royal Canadian Engineers proposed a scheme for converting a tank into an armoured vehicle for the use of engineers. It was felt that engineer personnel operating in conjunction with armoured formations should be provided with armour to protect and carry their stores. Comparative trials carried out with Shermans and Rams showed the value of the Ram's side doors for easy access to and exit from the vehicle under fire.

However, the Ram lacked stowage space, and the Churchill was considered a more suitable vehicle for the purpose. Its side (or pannier) doors were also at a more convenient height for access and the vehicle offered superior armour protection compared with the Ram or Sherman. In October 1942 orders were given to the 1st Canadian ME Coy to carry out a full conversion on an old 2pdr-armed Churchill incorporating all of Donovan's proposals. All ammunition bins were removed as well as the co-driver's seat, the turret basket and the main armament. New stowage compartments were fitted to take up 36 cubic ft of engineers' stores – demolition gear and tools, etc – and a mock-up of a spigot mortar, then under development, was fitted in the turret. The prototype was completed by December 1942.

Work on the actual spigot mortar prototype which was to arm this vehicle was commenced in September 1942. A preliminary experimental model was mounted and tested in a Covenanter tank and, as this proved successful, arrangements were made in November 1942 for the construction of three more weapons for installation in the Churchill engineer vehicle. So modified, the vehicle was known as an Armoured Vehicle Royal Engineers, AVRE for short. The new mortar was called a Petard and the bomb which this weapon projected was called a 'Flying Dustbin'. The Petard was designed to fit straight onto the 2pdr gun mantlet of the Churchill.

As a result of the inspection of the first AVRE prototype it was decided that the 1st ME Coy should go ahead and make a second prototype, this time converting a 6pdr-armed vehicle. This second prototype, slightly modified and without a gun, was ready by February 1943, trials being carried out late that month. On this occasion the first AVRE fired its Petard mortar for the first time and successfully demolished some concrete obstacles with the 'Flying Dustbin' bomb. Since it was desirable to convert Churchill IIIs and IVs as operational AVREs, it was decided to modify the Petard for fitting to the 6pdr mantlet.

Trials continued through 1943; the Petard design was finalised in March, the AVRE design in December, and immediate approval was given for production.

Early in 1944 it was decided to form and equip three RE regiments as armoured assult regiments for participation in Operation Overlord, the Normandy landings. These regiments were equipped with the first AVREs to be produced and formed the 1st Assult Brigade, RE, of 79th Armoured Division which had been formed under the command of Major-General (later Sir) P.C.S. Hobart, a veteran Tank Corps officer, to train and administer all the special purpose armour taking part in the invasion. In all, 180 Churchill Mks III and IV were modified by divisional workshops to AVRE configuration in the two months preceding D-Day. At the same time further modifications had been incorporated, as the result of the trials, to enable the AVRE to take such devices as fascines, bridges, and ploughs. Subsequently, in 1944-45, another 574 Churchills were converted to AVREs by MG at Abingdon (plates 42 et seq).

The Standard AVRE

As put into production in early 1944, the AVRE consisted of a basic Churchill III or IV with the 6pdr gun, cradle, elevating gear, and recoil system removed. Also removed were the ammunition stowage bins and co-driver's seat. The flaps of the co-driver's hatch were welded up and an aperture 13in x 12½in was cut out immediately above the co-driver's and fitted with a sliding flap. To load the Petard, the turret was traversed to bring the weapon above this aperture, whereupon the co-driver pushed the flap forward and passed a 'Flying Dustbin' up into the loading trough of the Petard. Compartments for holding the 'Flying Dustbins' each of about 9 cubic ft capacity, were formed in the side panniers fore and aft of the nearside escape door and aft of the offside door (plates 46, 47, 48)

Other equipment carried included electric cable which could be connected to the vehicle battery for firing the Wade charges and various types of associated demolition charge carried in the vehicle. The Petard was bolted direct to the 6pdr mantlet and fitted with a screw elevating gear suspended from gimbals on a bracket welded to the turret roof. The lower splash plate was modified to accommodate the Petard while the upper splash plate was completely redesigned. Fitments were added to the hull for the attachment of the various devices described separately below. Brief AVRE specification was as follows: Crew 6 (commander, demolition NCO, mortar gunner, wireless operator, driver, and co-driver/mortar loader); weight 38tons stowed; armament, one Mortar, recoiling, spigot 29mm Mk I or II; length of weapon 7ft 2in overall, loading trough 3ft 9in; demolition bomb 40lb, firing rate 2−3 rounds per minute; effective range with 40lb bomb, 80 yards. One Besa machine gun in hull. The 6pdr gunsight was retained for the Petard.

Right: the first Churchill tank to mount a 75mm gun was the Churchill IV(NA 75), a field conversion used in Italy which utilised an ex-Sherman (M4) tank gun. **Below right;** Churchill IVs carry infantry forward to the assault during the offensive on Caen in August 1944. The white tape indicates a swept path through a minefield.

For towing fascines, explosives, and other engineer stores, a simple drop-side sledge, known as the AVRE sledge, with steel runners was produced.

AVREs equipped the 5th Assault Regt, RE, the 6th Assault Regt, RE, and the 42nd Assault Regt, RE, these regiments together forming the 1st Assault Brigade, RE, for the invasion of Europe in June 1944. As finalised the AVRE design allowed for the fitting of numerous special devices and equipments for tackling the obstacles and defences likely to be encountered by the armoured units of 21 Army Group. The various equipments were as follows.

Fascines

These were developed for ditch crossing and consisted of brushwood bundles of two types, 6ft and 8ft in diameter, and 11ft long. They were carried on the front of the tank, supported by a wooden or steel cradle and could be jettisoned by a quick release mechanism which was operated by a line which led inside the tank through the cupola. In most cases a crewman had to expose himself to give directions to the driver, so experiments were carried out with periscopes similar to those used in the DD tanks; these were 6ft and 8ft in size and were fitted to the commander's cupola to enable the commander to see over the fascine. Trials were carried out late in 1944 with these periscopes (plate 45) but were later cancelled with the advent of new types of fascines which gave a better view ahead. The fascine itself was not a new idea and similar devices had been used with British tanks in World War I.

Dumbell Fascine (plate 49): various improved fascines were experimented with; one type known as the Dumbell Fascine was constructed with 'Christchurch Cribs' (bridging cribs) and chespale bundles to form the shape of a Dumbell. The weight of this was 2½ tons, length 12ft and diameter 8ft 6in. It saw limited post-war use.

Moyens Fascine Launcher (plate 57): this was an attempt to develop standard fascine equipment suitable for all tanks, by mounting the fascine on the turret instead of on the bow. A simple steel framework was fitted to the turret of the AFV, this supporting the fascine. The whole assembly could be traversed by revolving the turret. Due to its high and unwieldly nature, this device was not adopted.

Assault bridges

Mk II SBG: this device was evolved by the Canadian Army in April 1943 as a method for wall or ditch crossing in assault. A standard box girder bridge was fitted to the front of the AVRE and was adapted for quick release. For this conversion of the chassis, the holes in the inner horn plates for the Hollebone drawbar eyes were burnt out and bushes of 3in bore were welded in to take the pins of the SBG bridge bracket. This bridge weighed four tons, was 34ft long, and was controlled by a winch mounted on the rear of the vehicle. The bridge could surmount a 15ft wall or span a 30ft gap. Fascines were often used in conjunction with the SBG bridge. To enable AFVs to climb over high obstacles, the AVRE released its bridge at an angle, against the obstacle and then withdrew.

A second AVRE carrying a fascine climbed to the top of the bridge and dropped its fascine over the side of the wall; this broke the fall of the AVRE as it followed the fascine over the wall. The SBG had a 10ft track, took almost one minute to emplace and was rated as a Class 40 structure.

Towed Standard Box Girder Bridge: the towed SBG was a post-war (1948) development in which a normal SBG assault bridge was mounted on a detachable two-wheeled axle and trailed behind the AVRE by a detachable towing hook. This was a method of taking an SBG bridge over a long distance without placing strain on the AVRE, also improving the vision of the driver and therefore increasing the speed of the tank, and making it possible to pass under low bridges. The bridge when required could be picked up by the AVRE with SBG bracket winch and crane.

Folding SBG Assault Bridge: this device was another post-war refinement in which a normal assault bridge was modified so that it folded in the middle. The rear end of the bridge was attached to the AVRE in the normal manner. In the carrying position the bridge was folded and lashed together by cordage, which was cut before lowering. When launched the bridge was lowered by releasing the winchbrake and the bridge opened itself as it was lowered, this opening being effected by two fixed cables that pulled on a curved eagle frame attached to each side of the far half of the bridge.

Mat Laying Devices

The various mat-laying devices were evolved for laying rapidly and, if necessary, under fire a carpet in a lane over poor ground and over barbed-wire obstacles for trucks and infantry. One such device, as stated in the previous chapter, was first tried out at Dieppe; this consisted of a small bobbin fixed to the front of the Churchill, but with no side arms. This was an extemporised arrangement, however, apparently devised by the Canadian engineer staffs involved in planning the raid. The British were meanwhile developing a series of more sophisticated mat layers under the auspices of the Ministry of Supply and (later) 79th Armoured Division. In order of appearance, these were:

TLC Laying Device and Carpet (plate 58): This device consisted of a reinforced Hessian carpet wound on to a horizontal reel and carried above the ground, across the front of the Churchill by fixed side arms attached to the vehicle. Its primary object was to enable wheeled vehicles and infantry to cross barbed-wire obstacles. On meeting such an obstacle the weighted free end of the carpet was dropped onto the ground whilst the tank ran on to the free end, and then the carpet automatically unwound itself, so that the vehicle ran over it across the obstacle. On completion of the crossing the device could be jettisoned. This device was first tried out in March 1939 on a Cruiser Mk (A9), further trials being carried out on Matilda II tank and a Universal Carrier. Development of this device for fitment to the Churchill began in April 1942, the pilot model being tested in July. Production was completed by the end of 1944.

TLC Laying Device and Carpet, Fascine Type (plate 60): developed in 1940, this device was designed for rapidly laying a carpet in a lane over poor ground breached through a minefield. It was intended to be used for wheeled traffic only, but in emergency could be used by tracked vehicles. The carpet consisted of coir-chespale with 2in tubular reinforcement, 11ft wide and 100ft long. The carpet was tightly reeled in the shape of a fascine and mounted on a modified steel fascine cradle in a manner similar to the normal fascine. The carpet reel was held on the cradle by a set of travelling cables, and a reel spindle securing cable. The reel when released rotated on an axle through which the spindle securing cable was threaded. The carpet skidded out from underneath and dropped under the tracks of the AVRE. Laying speed was 5mph.

Log Carpet Device: the carpet consisted of 100 logs each 14ft long with an average diameter of 6-8in joined together by 2in wire rope. It was mounted on a steel frame on top of the AVRE. This framework consisted of Decauville Track fitted in sockets on the side of the AVRE, six on either side. The superstructure could be removed when not required. To release the log mat a series of small charges were fired which cut the cables holding the mat on the frame. Laying speed was 2mph.

Twin Bobbins (plate 59): This device had two small bobbins of Hessian and chespaling on a horizontal spindle carried across the front of the vehicle by fixed side arms attached to the tank, similar to the TLC equipment.

While all these types of equipment were produced they were mainly used for training. The TLC devices were evolved before the AVRE appeared and were seen fitted both to Churchill gun tanks and (later) AVREs. It was 79th Armoured Division who produced the most effective designs of mat layers, the Bobbins.

Bobbins: prior to the invasion of Normandy, aerial reconaissance had shown that some beaches had strips of blue clay in which vehicles would get bogged. A similar beach was found at Brancaster in Norfolk and a special trials wing was established there. As a result of these trials a few AVREs were equipped with bobbins on which were wound coir and tubular-scaffolding carpets. Used at Normandy, they were Bobbins Mk I (plate 61) and Mk II (plate 62) which were developed by the 79th Armoured Division trials wing in March 1943. They both carried a mat 9ft 1 lin in width but the Mk II carried longer lengths on movable arms. Operating speed was 2mph and the bobbin could be jettisoned by a small charge when expended.

Mine Rollers

Tanks with anti-mine roller devices were not intended to act in the capacity of minesweepers but were designed to protect other tanks (eg, flails) fitted for mine clearing against undetected mines and to assist tanks to cross small minefields. The rollers were positioned in front of each track of the vehicle using the device with the object of protecting the track, but it did not clear a broad enough path for other vehicles to follow unless several roller-fitted tanks were used in an overlapping echelon, which was generally impractical under combat conditions. Various anti-mine roller devices were tested on the heavily armoured Churchill, some of them being put into limited production.

AMRA Mk IIe : anti-mine roller devices were originally projected about 1937, prototypes being made by the firm of J. Fowler & Co of Leeds. One of these constructed by Messrs Fowler was tried out on a Medium Dragon Mk III/L and consisted of four rollers trailed, two in line with each track, from a frame attached to the vehicle. Development continued throughout the period 1937-43. Known as 'Fowler Rollers' the official designation was Anti-Mine Roller Attachment (AMRA). In order to indicate the small variations or modifications that had to be incorporated in the device so that it could be fitted to different types of tanks, the following nomenclature was used: AMRA Mk Ia for Matilda, AMRA Mk Ib for Valentine, AMRA Mk Ic for Convenanter, AMRA Mk Id for Crusader, and AMRA Mk IIe for the Churchill. The device consisted of a framework and suspension carried on spring-mounted and castoring rollers positioned in front of each track. It was attached to the tank by two brackets bolted to each side of the tank as shown in the accompanying diagram. When more than one roller had been blown off, the AMRA could be jettisoned. The Mk IIe device varied in basic design from the Mk I series, in that it had double roller forecarriage assemblies in place of single roller assemblies, this being due to the wider nature of the Churchill track. To guard against the possibility of the double rollers passing one each side of a mine the gap between the rollers was covered by a cast steel wheel called the 'Disc Coulter', one of which was fitted each side behind the roller assemblies. The weight of the Mk II device was 55 cwt compared with 30 cwt of the Mk Ia device (plate 74).

AMRCR: the Anti-Mine Reconnaissance Castor Roller Device (AMRCR) was a heavier and modified version of the AMRA and was tested in July 1943. The initial design of roller proved ineffective against German Teller mines so a new type of roller, made up of four 26in diameter steel discs interleaved with 22in diameter iron discs, was evolved by the Obstacle Assault Centre to replace the original solid design. After extensive trials a total of 60 AMRCRs were put into production. Like the AMRA this was a perambulator device attached to, and pushed in front of, the tank. It consisted of a framework and suspension carried on spring-mounted and castoring rollers positioned in front of each track. Four rollers, two in line with each track, were carried on an axle supported at either end by quarter elliptic leaf springs clamped to a transverse swivel axle immediately in front of the roller. The swivel axle was mounted at its centre on a vertical spindle, so as to have limited rotation about a longitudinal axis. The complete assembly was attached to the tank by two brackets bolted to each side. A release gear that could be operated from within the tank was incorporated. The weight of each roller was 16 cwt and the total weight of the device was 5 tons 4½ cwt. The AMRCR No 1, Mk I, could be fitted to all marks of Churchill (plates 75 and 76), and the No 1A, Mk I, was adapted for attachment to the Sherman V (M4A4). A scheme was later developed by which the AMRCR could be towed behind the vehicle when not required for its normal use in front of the tank.

CIRD: the CIRD (Canadian Indestructible Roller Device) was initiated by the Canadian Army, the prototype being built in 1943 at a Canadian Army workshop in the UK. It was a heavy type of roller designed to rotate about a bar after exploding a mine. Various sizes of roller were tested, but the CIRD was not developed in time to be produced in quantity before the end of the war. The CIRD followed the same principle as the AMRA and AMRCR, being a perambulator device attached to and pushed in front of the tank. It consisted of two rollers which were attached to their axle-pins to separate forks, bolted and welded in each case to a roller arm. Each roller was positioned in front of either tank track. The roller arms were located by two springs on a cross-bar which was mounted in two side arms, each secured to the hull by a fulcrum pin which, in turn, was mounted on a fulcrum bracket attached to the hull of the vehicle.

When a roller passed over a mine — which it detonated by its weight — the blast from the explosion threw the roller up into the air causing it to describe an arc about the cross-bar. This circular movement sent the roller in front of the cross-bar and the spade end of the roller arm dug into the ground. The forward movement of the tank forced the spade to act as a pivot or sprag and the cross-bar momentarily rode on the spade point forcing the cross-shaft and side arms to lift so that the roller returned once more to its normal trailing position. Operating speed of the CIRD was 5-6mph.

CIRD 16inch: preliminary development of this device took place in the summer of 1943. It was conceived by General Worthington, commander of the 4th Canadian Division and developed by Colonel Inglis in conjunction with the Obstacle Assault Centre (OAC). By October 1943, a prototype on a Churchill tank was tested (plate 77), this device having two solid armour plate rollers 26in in diameter by 16in wide and weighing one ton. In the following December a similar device was tested on a Sherman tank.

CIRD 15½in: serious defects occured with the 16in rollers, chief among them being the dropping of the side arms and the spreading of the rollers on mine detonation so that they jammed in the saddle and would not rotate. It was decided to reduce the width of the rollers from 16in to 15½in, and this took place in June 1944.

CIRD 18in: In order to improve mine detonating, efficiency trials were carried out on rollers 28in in diameter by 18in wide, running on 5ft diameter axles and weighing 3,000lb. These were approved for fitment to the Churchill device in August 1944. New redesigned side arms were also fitted (plates 78 and 79). The 18in CIRD was also adapted for the Sherman tank.

CIRD 21in: as it was considered that an even heavier roller than the 18in wide one might give improved protection to the 22in side track of the Churchill tank, tests were initiated in November 1944 on a roller 21in wide by 30in in diameter and weighing 4,100lb. As this 21in roller showed little improvement over the 18in roller and also imposed a strain on the engine clutch, tests were teminated in May 1945.

Limited production of the 16in and 18in CIRDs was undertaken, the first (16in) equipment being delivered in April 1944. The firms of Edwin Danks, Oldbury, and H. Simon, Cheadle Heath, shared the contract.

Fittings, consisted of bolt holes and shoe plates, were provided on the hull sides of all except the earliest production AVREs to allow attachment of all CIRD, AMRA, and AMRCR arms. It took only about 10 minutes to actually attach roller equipment to an AVRE though there was always the time and trouble involved in transporting it to the scene of operations which mitigated against its use. So far as is known, CIRD was never used in the field, and the others only rarely so.

Mine Ploughs

For mine clearance in assault in areas where the exploding of the mines would crater the ground and render it impassable to traffice, a form of tank-propelled plough was evolved which could uproot and sweep the mines aside so that they could later be collected and rendered safe by sappers. Various types of ploughs were developed and experimented with, having mixed combinations of ploughshares and rollers. One such equipment, the Bullshorn Mk III, (plate 68) was used successfully by the 5th Assault Regt. RE, at Lion-Sur-Mer, where they cleared the minefields on the beaches and between the houses on the sea front. The Obstacle Assault Centre (OAC) was instrumental in evolving most of the plough equipment in conjunction with 79th Armoured Division. All the devices they designed could be fitted to the Churchill AVRE and, in some cases, to the Sherman. In mid 1943 the OAC tested the various designs they had in mind. These were known for test purposes as Ploughs A-D and brief details are given, together with names later adopted in parentheses.

Plough A (OAC Mk I): consisted of a combination unit of ploughshares and twin rollers each unit positioned in front of the tank track. The two units were attached to a girder frame, this frame having a counterweight structure (plate 63).

Plough B (Bullshorn Mk II): consisted of a large centre curved plate flanked either side by a ploughshare, the whole assembly being mounted on a girder frame, with the side arms of the frame counterweighted (plate 64).

Plough C (OAC Mk II): similar to Plough A but the units of twin rollers were replaced by two heavy rollers, and the counterweight girders were replaced by weights (plate 66).

Plough D: this was made up of two ploughs attached to a heavy short girder frame which was controlled by a Atherton jib crane *(qv)* mounted at the rear of the tank (plate 65).

Senior Equitine Cultivator: this was a wheeled farm cultivator towed behind an AVRE device to lift mines. It was tested with Ploughs A-D as a possible alternative idea.

Harrow: this was a similar device to the Senior Equitine Cultivator, consisting of a wheeled farm harrow towed behind a Churchill. Again, it was tested against Ploughs A-D to investigate the feasibility of utilising readily available agricultural implements for minesweeping (plate 67).

Bullshorn Plough (plate 68): consisted of ploughshares mounted on a girder frame set in front of the vehicle. Variations existed of this equipment. Bullshorn Mk III was evolved in March 1944, by the 79th Armoured Division. The weight of this plough equipment was 11cwt 2qtr, operating speed 4mph and the area cleared 2ft 9in, this being the tank track ground only. It was developed from the original Plough B.

Jeffries Plough: this was similar to the Bullshorn Plough, but somewhat simplified (plate 69).

Farmer Front: developed in mid 1943, it was designed for fitment to the Churchill AVRE by means of the same brackets as used for the AMRCR. The device consisted of 19 lines in arrowhead formation in front of the tank, the framework supported by three 3ft wheels and two 4ft 6in wheels (plate 70).

Farmer Track: this was developed in late 1943. The frame of this device was attached to the Churchill in the same way as the main top frame of the Farmer Front. Its weight was taken at the forward end by two 5ft diameter wheels, 15in wide within the frame, one in front of either track. In front and as close as possible to each wheel were 6 curved tines positioned in arrowhead formation (plate 71).

Farmer Deck: the frame of this device was of lattice construction and a short plough was positioned in front of each track. The whole assembly was counterweighted on either side of the vehicle by a heavy girder (plates 72, 73).

Farmer Deck IIIA: this device was developed in August 1943, and consisted of two large ploughshares mounted, one in front of either track in a frame connected by a pivot to the tank at the rear and supported at the front on rollers.

Charge Placers

To enable obstacles to be breached or demolished and at the same time give maximum protection to the demolition personel, several Mechanical Charge Placers were evolved and experimented with. These were essentially suspended explosive charges on frames mounted in front of the tank for placing in front of or across the obstacles to be demolished. Because of its heavy armour, stable chassis, and adoption as the standard AVRE, the Churchill was the carrier vehicle used for almost all British developed explosive charge devices.

The Light Carrot: developed in July, 1942, this was a name given to an elongated rectangular explosive charge carried on a frame mounted on the nose of the tank so that it could be positioned against the object to be breached and fired from within the tank without exposure of the tank crew. Charges from 12lb to a maximum of 25lb could be carried on these extended brackets without danger to the crew (plate 81). Trials were also carried out with heavier charges up to 660lb mounted on the top front frame of the Anti-Mine Roller Attachment (AMRA 1a) device fitted to the Matilda tank; this device was known as the Heavy Carrot.

Onion (Jones Onion): developed in August 1942, this device (plate 82) consisted of 1,000lb HE charges fitted to a framework attached to the front of the tank. The framework measured 9ft wide by 4ft 6in high. It was carried vertically by two side arms attached one each side of the vehicle. When the tank with the explosive device arrived at the obstacle to be attacked a mechanical release cable was pulled allowing the frame of charges to fall. A pair of cranked legs pivoted to the frame met the ground first, so that the frame fell forward and was retained against the obstacle. The tank was then reversed away and the charges fired electrically by a trailing cable. Trials were also made with a similar smaller device, this being known as the Single Onion (plate 83).

Quinson Device: this was another form of explosive frame for hanging on an obstacle and was carried vertically on two side arms attached one each side of the vehicle (plate 84).

Goat Mk III: a further development of the Carrot and Onion devices. The Goat was carried horizontally in the front of the tank and was so designed that contact with a wall or obstacle automatically placed the explosive frame into position. This device was put under development in October, 1943, and by January 1944 had resulted resulted in the Goat Mk III, some 400 of which were produced (plate

Above left; a REME recovery crew with a Churchill ARV I (Background) give assistance to a mined Churchill VI during the Caumont offensive of July 1944. The swept path is indicated by the tapes in the background. **Below left;** a 79th Armoured Division assault group consisting of an AVRE (left) and two Churchill Crocodiles (centre, and trailer visible far right) move forward to tackle an enemy strong point while operating in support of American troops (foreground). France, November 1944.

85). For this device 1,800lb of explosive charges were fitted to a platform 10ft 6in wide by 6ft 6in long. The frame was carried in a horizontal position above the nose of the AVRE in such a way that the platform was nose heavy. The weight of the platform was mainly taken by two struts attached one each side of the front of the hull. A release mechanism was fitted between the rear of the platform and the top of the hull vizor plate and this retained the platform in position. Two antennae, spring loaded and retained by shear wires, projected horizontally ahead of the platform. When the antennae made contact with the obstacle, the shear wires broke allowing the antennae to spring backwards, thereby operating the quick release mechanism so that the front of the platform tilted forward and downwards. at the same time two sprags hinged on either side of the rear end of the platform were released. The tank then pushed the explosive platform vertically up against the obstacle and backed off. The platform was now retained in its position by the two sprags. When the tank was clear of the obstacle the charges were fired either electrically or by pull igniter.

Elevatable Goat: this device was for use against high walls or obstacles and consisted of a long braced frame carried on the nose of the AVRE in a similar manner to the Assault SBG. Fitted under the two main spars were a series of linked charges. On approaching the obstacle the complete assembly was placed against the wall and jettisoned from the vehicle. The linked charges were next released and these fell away from the spars and lay across the wall. The tank then withdrew and the charges were blown (plate 87).

Bangalore Torpedo: this device consisted of two lengths of Snake piping fitted to a Onion frame assembly on the front of the AVRE. In limited service, it was for use against light obstacles and barbed wire (plate 88).

Mine Clearing Devices

3in Snake: developed in August 1942 and used operationally in Italy, this device consisted of 20ft lengths of 3in water piping filled with explosives, 16 lengths being carried on the Churchill. These were carried 8 per side over the tracks, being laid on short girder sections. The pipes were fitted together and pushed or pulled by the vehicle into the minefield, released and then detonated, the blast creating a path approximately 21ft wide. Maximum pushing length was 400ft and for towing 1,200ft. Pushing speed was 2-8 mph according to terrain. Extra explosive piping was carried by a 3ton truck (plates 89, 90 and 91).

Churchill Gun Carrier with 3in Snake: this was an experiment to adapt the obsolet Gun Carrier *(qv)* as a carrier vehicle for Snake. The 3in gun was removed and 25 lengths of snake were packed either side of the fixed turret, being retained in this position by two metal bars fitted either side of the vehicle. Used as described above, but tested only.

Conger 2in Mk I: evolved in January 1944 for mine clearance in assault, this consisted of an engineless carrier containing a 5in Rocket No 3 Mk I and projector, air bottles, and a tank of explosive. Fitted to the rear of the carrier was a wooden box containing 330yards of 2in woven hose. The explosive carrier was towed to the edge of the minefield and released. The empty hose was attached to the rocket and fired over the minefield so that it lay extended across the field, one end still being connected to the carrier. The hose was then pumped full of explosive by compressed air. When sufficient explosive had been pumped into the hose, the carrier was removed and the hose was detonated by a delay pull igniter, the blast blowing a path through the field. This equipment saw limited operational use (plate 92).

Giant Viper: this was a postwar version of the Conger. The explosive filled hose was loaded in a specially built trailer hauled by which also carried launching rockets for projecting the hose. The trailer was towed to the edge of the minefield by a Churchill AVRE where the line charge was then launched across the field by a rocket towing unit. When the hose had reached the end of its launch it was lowered to the ground by parachutes where it was detonated. This device remains in use in conjunction with the Centurion AVRE (plate 93).

Rocket Mine Clearance Device: this consisted of a number of 5in Rockets mounted on a light frame that was fitted at an angle on the nose of the Churchill. It was developed to investigate the possibility of clearing a lane through a minefield by means of air blast. A postwar idea, it was not proceeded with.

AVRE Projects

Ardeer Aggie: owing to a demand for a more powerful demolition weapon than the Petard, the Ardeer Aggie was proposed. Originally called the Ardeer projector, it was a recoilless gun in which the recoil momentum was neutralised by the firing of a dummy projectile at the rear simultaneous with the discharge of the main projectile through the barrel. Development work on this weapon was started in september 1943, the first prototype being mounted on a 6pdr field carriage. The second Ardeer prototype was mounted on a Churchill III in 1944. It weighed 9cwt and had a length of 10ft. The projectile weighed 54lb and the sand-filled dummy counter-projectile weighed 48lb. Range was 450years and the rate of fire about three rounds in two minutes. Development of this interesting weapon was stopped as it was found to be impractical under combat conditions (plates 51,52).

Woodpecker: this was another experimental version of the AVRE evolved during 1944 for the demolition of concrete fortifications, and consisted of 'Flying Dustbins' with rocket attachments mounted, four each side of the vehicle. They could be fired in salvo or as single shots. A disadvantage was the lack of reloading facilities from inside the vehicle.

4.
Special Purpose Types and Equipment

Flamethrowers

The first type of Churchill flamethrower was the Oke which was used experimentally at Dieppe (as already recorded) and had been developed by the Petroleum Warfare Dept in order to test flamethrowing ideas under combat conditions. The Oke was fitted with a Ronson flame gun with a fixed elevation so that it could only be aimed by manoeuvring the tank; range was 40-50yds and the flame fuel was carried in jettisonable tanks mounted at the rear. The normal gun armament was carried. In the event, none of the three vehicles so fitted survived long enough to see action at Dieppe. The PWD developed the Oke in a hurry, bypassing usual channels for procuring new types (plates 20 and 21).

The Crocodile (plates 40 and 41), which was the best known and most famous of all flamethrowing tanks had a happier story and was destined to win great fame in the NW Europe campaign as one of the most formidable of the weapons used to breach the 'West Wall'. Development started in 1941 when the Petroleum Warfare Department produced two types of flamethrowing projectors. one operated by cordite charges, the other by gas pressure. Both were tried experimentally in Valentine tanks. After trials with the prototypes, the General Staff decided to standardise on the gas-operated projector and an installation was made on a Churchill tank. Experiments took place throughout 1942 and the design was finalised and placed in production in 1943. It was decided to use the Churchill VII as the standard Crocodile vehicle and sufficient were ready to take part in the D-Day landings. These did useful work on burning out beach defences and pill boxes and subsequent notable Crocodile operations included the assault on the Siegfried Line. Some were also used in Italy.

The Crocodile equipment consisted of an armoured two-wheel trailer weighing 6½tons and containing 400gallons of flame fuel, controls, and five pressure bottles containing nitrogen. Connection from trailer to flame projector in the tank hull was through the Link, a device through which pressurised fuel could pass. A range of 120yards was obtainable in favourable conditions but the generally accepted range was 80yards. The projector could fire 80 one-second bursts on continuous fire. If the trailer was hit or damaged it could be jettisoned by a quick release device and the tank — which retained its main armament — reverted to its usual role as a gun tank. The flame projector took the place of the hull machine gun and was operated by the hull gunner. The Churchill Crocodile weighed 41.2 tons.

A further Churchill flamethrower project was the Cobra, also known as the Mamba. This was a device for fitting in the field and the project was intended for Far East operations in 1945. A 180 gallon fuel tank pressure bottle, and controls were carried on the hull rear and the fuel passed alongside the off-side through an armoured cover pipe. The projector was fitted on a turntable above the co-driver's hatch. The Cobra never saw service, in fact due to the cessation of hostilities. The equivalent equipment on the British Sherman was called the Adder.

Recovery Vehicles

Production of a recovery vehicle, the Churchill ARV Mk I, was begun in February 1942, the basic vehicle being a Churchill II with the turret and armament removed. A portable jib crane with a lifting capacity of 5 tons was fitted so that it could be easily erected, and gas cutting and welding equipment with tools and repair equipment was stowed in the hull. A crew of 3 was carried including the driver. The ARV Mk I was primarily an armoured tug, having a drawbar connector fitted at the rear. The jib booms were carried on the sides and when required they were mounted on the front of the vehicle and raised by a wire rope clamped to the track. The chain block carried at the head of the boom was capable of a 3 ton lift. Armament consisted of a 7.92mm Besa machine gun in the hull, and two Bren or Sten guns. Weight was 33 tons (plate 53).

The Churchill ARV Mk II was based on the Churchill Mk IV chassis, the standard turret being replaced by a fixed turret fabricated from 40mm armoured plate welded to the roof of the vehicle, with a turret roof of 14mm plate carrying two cupolas. A dummy 6pdr gun was mounted, though some later vehicles had a dummy 75mm gun.

The special equipment carried consisted of a dismountable forward or front jib capable of supporting a 7½ ton load, a fixed rear jib for lifting or giving a combined lift and haul of 15 tons, and a two-speed winch driven from the engine capable of developing a direct pull of 25 tons through the winch rope which passed from a drum through a rectangular opening in the rear plate of the turret with suitable guide rollers. A spade-type earth anchor was hinged at the rear of the vehicle to prevent rearward movement of the vehicle when the winch pull exceeded the tractive resistance of the AFV. Miscellaneous equipment and tools including 25 ton snatch blocks, shackles, tow ropes, and gas welding equipment was carried for the crew of 4. The weight of the vehicle was 40.1 tons. Armament consisted of one 7.92mm Besa in the hull and one Bren gun (plates 55,56).

There was also an experimental Churchill BARV which was an adapted version of the ARV I, for beach recovery, the requirement being initiated in Spring 1943 during planning for the invasion of France. Shingle plates were fitted over the bogie assembly and wading gear was installed as required (plate 54). This project was swiftly abandoned October 1943 in favour of the Sherman BARV, the Sherman proving much superior for beach operations.

Bridge Carriers

Experiments with bridges or ramps to be carried by tanks were first undertaken during the latter part of World War I. During this period trials took place with a Mark V* carrying a girder structure mounted on its nose which could be laid to span a 20ft gap. Further trials of bridging devices were made in the mid-twenties, the carrying vehicle being a Dragon Mk I with a 30ft bridge mounted on its modified structure. The bridge was launched by a pulley system. The Vickers

Medium Tank Mk II was also adapted and carried two 18ft ramps on either side of the hull, these being hinged and folded back and supported by brackets fixed on the hull side. When required the Medium Tank device had to be manhandled into position.

Interest in self-propelled bridging equipment seems to have waned until the outbreak of World War II, and with the lessons learnt at Dieppe began the evolvement of a new series of projects. These fell into two groups — ramps that utilised the hull of the tank as a part of the device, and mobile bridges which could be launched from the carrying vehicle. Most numerous were the ARKs, these initials being derived as an abbreviation from 'Armoured Ramp Carrier'.

Churchill ARK Mk I: the ARK I was a turretless Churchill tank on top of which were built two timbered runways along the length of the hull, one immediately above each track. A ramp was hinged to each trackway at the rear of the vehicle. The vehicle was intended to be driven up against a vertical wall with its nose held against it as high as possible, so that vehicles could climb up its ramps on the trackway and then on to and over the wall. Alternatively the ARK could be driven into an anti-tank ditch so that following vehicles could be driven over. The first expermental model of this equipment was developed by the 79th Armoured Division late in 1943, and owing to the promise shown by this project a requirement was put forward for 50 ARKs, arrangements being made in February 1944 to prepare a production design and two prototypes. The hulls used for the ARK conversion were Churchills II and IV that were originally earmarked for conversion to CDLs. Stowage and internal fittings were identical to those of the AVRE hull: the turret and turret basket were removed and part of the rotating base junction left exposed on the hull floor was enclosed by a spherical cover. Slight rearrangements of tow rope and exhaust system were necessitated by the presence of the trackways. The timbered trackway was raised above the hull by brackets and girders. Hinged to the front girders were two ramps 3ft 5¾in long, in line with each trackway. The front ends of these ramps rested on the tracks above the front idlers, whilst a projection on the underside of each ramp engaged the spuds of the track giving a ratchet action so that the tank could be driven forwards with the front ramp oscillating up and down. This feature assisted in maintaining the vehicle in an inclined position when driven up against a vertical wall. Two 5ft 8in ramps were hinged to the rear girders, so that when the vehicle was on level ground they hung vertically with their ends clear of the ground. The construction of the ramps was similar to the trackway portion of the main superstructure. The ARK I could also be used as an explosive carrier in a secondary role (plate 107).

Churchill ARK II (UK Pattern): at the end of July 1944 trials were carried out on an ARK I modified by the 79th Armoured Division. These modifications were made to the existing ARK to allow for the passage of 'B' vehicles over the ramps. As a result of these trials, arrangements were made for converting all existing ARK Is and ARK IIs. This consisted of various alterations to the trackway superstructure and included the widening of the left-hand trackway from 2ft to 4ft; the right hand trackway remained 2ft wide. Hinged to the front transoms were two short 3ft 7½in ramps, in line with each runway, to which in turn were hinged two ramps each 12ft 6in long. Two ramps, each 12ft 6in long were hinged to the rear end of the runway, all the ramps corresponding in width to the runways to which they were linked. The construction of the ramps was similar to that of the runways except in the case of the wide left-hand ramps, where three longitudinals were provided to accomodate the increased width. The ramps were initially raised from the stowed position and erected with the aid of a second vehicle and crane. In the erected position each rear ramp was supported by a ¾in diameter tie rod with eyes at both ends, connected to 2in diameter pins welded on the outside near end of the ramp. The other ends of the tie rods were held by plugs which formed tongues of quick-release blocks welded to the vehicle. The plugs could be withdrawn simultaneously by means of a quick release assembly operated from within the vehicle. To support the front ramps in the erected position a 12ft long post was fitted, and this was mounted on a pin passing through the existing front tow eye and an additional similar eye, welded on the nose plate adjacent to it. Welded at the upper end of the king post were brackets to which were shackled two 8ft long 5/8in diameter steel hawsers secured by shackles to brackets welded to the inside of the forward end of the front ramps. To secure the front ramps in the erected position a 3ft long 5/8in diameter steel hawser with a length of chain shackled to it at each end, was passed round a 5ton snatch block mounted at the upper end of the king post. One of the chains was passed through a 'U' bracket welded near the centre of the second transon from the front of the trackway, and secured by a shackle. The other was held by a Convenanter quick release hook was operated by a Bowden cable mechanism from within the vehicle. The turret aperture in the hull roof was covered by a 14mm thick blanking plate welded in position. This plate incorporated a double flap hatch cover giving access to the centre compartment. A rectangular conning tower was welded into position around the hatch and half the left-hand runway was removable to give access to the engine and transmission compartments. Some vehicles were fitted with independent release gear for each rear ramp. A wireless No 19 set was fitted in the right-hand pannier aft of the side door. The basic vehicles used for the ARK II conversions were Churchills III and IV. Crew was 4, and the weight was 38tons 10cwt. Trials were later carried out using 20ft long ramps.

Churchill ARK II (Italian Pattern): produced in Italy by the ME Forces, the Italian pattern of ARK II had the trackguards removed and utilised its own tracks as the fixed runway, crossing vehicles making direct contact with the tracks and roof plates, in contrast to the ARK II (UK Pattern) which had the built-up trackways. The gap between the front of the vehicle and the front ramps was covered by a platform extension instead of articulated short ramps as on the UK pattern vehicle. The front and rear ramps were of American origin (Treadway tracks) of equal length and interchangeable. Two different types could be used, the M1 which was 15ft 3in long and the M2, 12ft 3½in long. Two kingposts, one at either end, supported the ramps in the raised position and the quick release mechanism was mounted on the turret blanking plate, which was circular in shape. The external exhaust system was modified and flash eliminators were fitted. A wireless No 19 set was fitted in the left-hand pannier aft of the side door. Weight of this version was 39tons and a crew of 4 was carried (plate 109).

Churchill with Foldups: developed in 1945-46, this had a family resemblance to the ARK II. The ramps were original American trackway bridge, and were launched by rockets from the position in which they were folded on top of the ARK. This was experimental only.

Churchill IV Octopus: this was the Italian pattern ARK with modified folding ramps hinged in two places. Each ramp was 15ft long fully extended and the ramps were either hinged and folded on top of the vehicle or stowed separately and attached during bridging operations.

Churchill GE Ramp (Great Eastern): evolved for wall and ditch crossing in assault, trials of this device took place in May 1944, the basic vehicle being a Churchill I. As these trials proved successful a further 10 prototypes were made, this time the basic vehicles being Churchill IVs with the stronger Churchill VII suspension (plate 111). During 1945, these 10 vehicles were sent to 21 Army Group who put two on user trials, but due to the lack of requirements for this type of device, the Great Eastern project was dropped. The GE Ramp, was basically similar to the ARK and consisted of a 27ft long superstructure built on the turretless Churchill IV. Hinged to and folded back to the superstructure was a 5 ton, 25 ft long ramp, which was raised and propelled into position by two groups of 3in electrically fired rockets that were fitted to the ramp's free ends. Also fitted were two concertina shock absorber boxes to absorb the impact of the falling ramps. The rear 2 ton 13ft ramp was set into the dropping position and released by means of electrically operated blow-out pins. Following vehicles could then mount the rear ramp and cross the operating vehicle.

Lakeman ARK (Gun Churchill): evolved in 1944 for wall crossing, this experimental device consisted of a combat Churchill with a sloping superstructure built on its hull. Attached to the rear of the superstructure which sloped down to the the back of the vehicle was attached a hinged ramp. The vehicle approached its position in front of the wall, dropped its ramp, and the following vehicles climbed on to the ramp, crossed over the built-up superstructure and on to the wall (plate 110).

Churchill Woodlark: this consisted of a turretless Churchill tank upon which was mounted a girder superstructure and trackways similar to the ARKs. On top of the trackways were four folded ramps, each ramp hinged in three places. The object of the hinging was to allow the ramps to articulate in their working position and following the contours of the obstacle. The ramps were operated by rockets placed near the main hinges and at the end of the top sections. A set of quick-burning rockets was also placed in each ramp assembly so that the shock of impact would be reduced as the ramps were falling (plate 113).

Churchill Hudnott ARK: this was another device which incorporated rocket operating ramps. The ramps were mounted one on top of the other, with guide ways along the side, through which the ramps could be pulled by rockets. This existed as a project model only (plate 112).

Churchill Bridgelayer (Bridge, Tank, 30ft, No 2): evolved for ditch crossing in assault during 1942, this device consisted of a 30ft bridge carried on top of a turretless Churchill. When required the 4.8 ton bridge was lifted hydraulically on a pivot arm and placed forward across the gap to be bridged. The tank could also recover its bridge by the same process. The bridge was designed to carry a 60ton tracked vehicle or Class 40 wheeled vehicles, and consisted of two tracks of welded construction joined together by crosspieces. The laying mechanism was operated by the driver. Basic vehicles used were Churchills III and IV. Crew was 2 men only a driver and commander, and a special cupola was provided for the commander which was fitted with doors to provide entry into the tank. Weight of the complete vehicle and device was 40.8 tons. The hydraulic drive mechanism was carried in the original turret space. Production vehicles (by conversion from gun tanks) were ready in 1944 and were first used operationally in Normandy. The original establishment was one troop of three vehicles to each tank brigade, but later (and post-war) they were issued on a more generous scale. The Churchill Bridgelayer was one of the best and most effective of all bridging devices evolved during World War II and its design in turn was based on experience with the earlier Convenanter and Valentine Bridgelayers (plate 114).

Churchill Bridgelayer (Bridge, Tank, 30ft No. 3): this device was similar to Bridge Tank No 2 but the bridge was modified to carry the new types of heavier tracked vehicles that were coming into service in 1946. Weight of bridge was 5.2 tons. Later Churchill Bridgelayers (postwar) incorporated the Mk VII chassis. Both types remained in service postwar, seeing service in Korea, and not being finally withdrawn until the early sixties when the Centurion Bridgelayer became available (plate 115).

Churchill Skid Bailey: used in operations in Europe, this device consisted of a Bailey Bridge of certain length (depending on the gap to be bridged) assembled on skids near the site of operations. When erected the bridge was pushed or skidded (hence its name) by one or two Churchill AVREs fitted with nose attachments. As the bridge was built longer than the gap to be bridged, the gap was spanned by the main section of the bridge before the point of balance was reached. Typical use was for bridging large craters in roads under fire.

Churchill Mobile Bailey: this equipment was developed in the United Kingdom in 1943 and first used operationally in Italy in April 1945 at the crossing of the river Senio (plate 116). The Bailey Mobile Bridge was designed to be pushed as a complete class 40 bridge to a 70 or 80ft wide gap where it could be launched and opened to traffic within minutes. It was assembled a considerable distance from the site to be bridged to give protection to the bridge-building RE unit. The bridge consisted of 150ft span of Bailey Bridge fitted with 10ft hinged ramps at either end. When erected the centre of the bridge was mounted on two Orolo caterpillar tracks, which were tracked rollers but provided no power. An early type of this bridge used a turretless Churchill as the carrying vehicle instead of caterpillar units. The tail end of the bridge was connected to the nose of a Churchill AVRE by a frame. The assembled bridge was pushed up to and over the gap until the Orolo tracks had reached the edge and the main span of 90ft of bridging protruding in front of these tracks was placed across the gap. The pusher tank then withdrew, dropping the hinged ramp. An additional AVRE towed from the front on the approach to the site.

Churchill Mobile Brown Bridge: developed by Captain B.S. Brown, Royal Canadian Engineers, of the 8th Army in Italy, this bridge was based on an early improvisation that had been used for the assault crossing of the River Rapido in May 1944. The bridge consisted of 140ft of Bailey Bridge transported by two Churchill tanks, one of which had its turret removed. This, the carrier tank, was positioned slightly in front of the point of balance of the bridge taking the bulk of the load, this position being maintained while in transit. Fitted to the top deck of the carrier tank were a series of launching rollers upon which lay the bridge. The pusher tank fitted with attachments for holding and releasing the bridge was positioned below the rear transom, where a skeleton 30ft tail was attached. This false tail was designed to act as a counterweight (plate 117). To launch the bridge the vehicles carrying the bridge advanced towards the 80ft gap to be spanned. The carrier tank halted when the edge of the gap was reached, and the pusher tank continued to advance, and in doing so pushed the bridge over the rollers, that were fitted on the carrier tank. As the pusher tank closed up to the carrier tank, the gap was spanned; the pusher tank and the skeleton tail were then disengaged from the bridge and reversed away, being in turn followed by the carrier tank, the bridge sliding down the carrier rollers as it moved back.

Churchill Mobile Dalton Bridge: this device was developed by Major T.R. Dalton, RE, as an improvement on the Brown Bridge but was not used operationally. The 140ft of Bailey Bridge was carried on two tanks. The carrier tank, a Churchill Ark, was fitted with four transoms clamped laterally across the top deck, upon which mounted rocking rollers and guide rollers. The Ark was positioned a little forward of midpoint on the bridge to take about two-thirds of the total load, this portion of the bridge resting on the rollers. The pusher tank, a Churchill AVRE, was fitted with two special frames upon which were mounted winches. These were connected by tackle to the last trunnion of the bridge. The pusher frames were bolted to existing fittings at each side of the tank, and were arranged to form a tray, the horizontal members of which supported the bridge. Also attached to the rear of the bridge was a skeleton tail to act as a counterweight (plate 118). To launch the bridge, the two vehicles carrying the bridge advanced towards the site, and the carrier tank halted at the edge of the gap, while the pusher tank continued to move forward. In doing so, it pushed the bridge over the stationary carrier rollers until the nose of the bridge had reached the far side. The nose of the bridge had reached the far side. The nose of the bridge was then lowered to the ground by means of the winches on the pusher tank, which then disengaged by blowing with a small charge the links connecting the winch cables to the bridge. This vehicle then withdrew, followed by the carrier tank which backed out from under the bridge, lowering it to the ground as it passed from underneath.

Miscellaneous Projects

Churchill CDL: this was the Churchill with a specially designed armoured turret housing a searchlight (Canal Defence Light). It was originally planned to convert numbers of Churchill tanks to CDL vehicles but this was cancelled and the hulls that had been earmarked for this conversion were subsequently converted to ARKS *(qv)*. In the event the Grant tank was converted to form the main CDL type. Prototypes were completed and tested in 1943. Due to its relatively low speed it was found more vulnerable to anti-tank fire than other CDL types.

Churchill Pussyfoot: a modified engine and gearbox were fitted in 1942 to a Churchill, T32144, with rubber-typed bogies, in an attempt to give smoother running qualities. It was experimental only, the work being done by Vauxhall (plate 98).

Churchill with Assault Sledges: this was an experimental project for transporting assault troops in armoured one-man sledges towed behind the Churchill in units of four. A similar idea was tried with the Sherman. Tested in May 1943 these assault sledges proved effective in that they protected the occupants. However, they were also severely impractical and uncomfortable (plate 97).

Miscellaneous Equipment

Atherton Jack: this was a portable jib crane which could be mounted on the Churchill turret (and the turrets of other tanks). for engine changing or other maintenance tasks. It was normally used with a chain purchase (plate 94).

Transportable Derrick: this consisted of an electric powered jib fitted with two wheels and a detachable power unit. The assembly was towed behind the AVRE. When required the jib and its fixed wheels were mounted on the front of the vehicle, being connected to the existing AVRE fittings, and the portable power unit was attached to the rear of the vehicle where it controlled the Jib. The War Office requirement for this equipment for formulated in June 1944 and design was completed by May 1945. It saw limited production for use with the AVRE (plate 95).

Whyman Mechanical Lane Marking Device: evolved in 1944 for lane marking through minefields, it was fitted to Flail and AVRE tanks. It was also used for pegging down Bobbin mats that had been laid down over poor ground. The device consisted of two banks of 12 firing tubes mounted on each side at the rear of the tank. Each firing tube was fitted with a flagged picket, and at intervals a picket was fired into the ground by means of a ballistic cartridge. The 7ft long picket penetrated 12in into the ground and remained upright to display the flag and so mark the path that had been cleared (plate 96).

Centipede Rollers: evolved in 1943 for the clearance of small anti-personnel mines, the Centipede rollers consisted of 12 small rollers on parallel bars which could be towed behind the Churchill, Sherman, or other tanks engaged in mine clearing. Each roller was of concrete with a steel tyre and weighed 30lbs. The Centipede was used mainly to follow up flail tanks in a swept lane to detonate 'S' mines missed by the flails.

Churchill RYPA: this was an oscillating gun-platform with mock-up turret for training Churchill crews in gunnery.

Deep Wading Equipment: an early version of this equipment was first tried at Dieppe on the Churchills which came ashore from the LCTs. It was vastly improved on during the course of the war and came in kit form to provide trunking for radiator grilles, exhaust pipe extensions, and seals for all hull orifices.

5.
Projects and Prototypes

Though several new designs were projected at various times based on the Churchill, only two of these actually reached prototype and/or production status. As
early as Spring 1940 the Department of Tank Design drew up a scheme for a modified, lighter version of the A20 under the designation A21. However, work on this
ceased with the demise of the A20, although project drawings are known to have
been made.

A23 and A26

In January 1941 a cruiser tank version of the Churchill tank reached specification stage. At this time the Tank Board were considering proposals for a new
fast 'heavy cruiser' tank with 6pdr main armament to replace the A9, A10 and
A13 types which were undergunned, too lightly armoured, and generally outmoded. Three firms offered designs: Mechanisation and Aero, Birmingham Railway and Carriage Co, and Vauxhall. Vauxhall suggested a shorter lighter version
of the A22, designated A23, which would weigh 24tons and have a speed of 24-
mph. They reasoned that as standard A22 components would be used, production
could be started very quickly. However, the Tank Board favoured the other two
designs, the A24 (later the Cavalier) and A27 (later the Centaur/Cromwell) and no
development order was given to Vauxhall. Nonetheless, while the deliberations
were going on Vauxhall produced a modified form of the A23 project, the A26,
which differed principally in having armour thicknesses and turret ring diameter
altered to conform precisely with the Tank Board's requirements — 65mm hull
front, 75mm turret front, and 60in diameter turret ring. Like the A23 it
was shelved and no detailed design was worked out.

The 3in Gun Carrier

By Summer 1941 the British tank forces in the Western Desert had suffered
badly at the hands of Rommel's Afrika Korps. As a result of this the General Staff
asked the Tank Board to investigate the mounting of high velocity heavy calibre
guns in cruiser and infantry tanks to overcome what was considered to be a prime
failing in existing British tanks, lack of gun power. None in service at that time
had a gun larger than 2pdr and the 6pdr gun was only just going into production.
The Challenger was eventually produced after much development to meet the
cruiser tank requirement, but the infantry tank requirement offered its own problem. Neither of the existing infantry tanks, the Mk III (Valentine) and the Mk
IV (Churchill) would take a gun bigger than a 6pdr due to their narrow widths
which limited turret size. At the same time the proposed high velocity tank gun,

the 17pdr, was then only in the early design stage. It was therefore suggested that the 3in (21cwt) AA gun should be used until the 17pdr was ready, and could be fitted to the Churchill in a limited traverse mount 179 where turret size would no longer be a decisive factor. The 3in AA gun was available in some numbers as it had been recently replaced in AA units by the 3.7in gun.

Vauxhall were therefore asked in September 1941 to adapt the Churchill design to take the 3in guns and 100 of these weapons with special 12½lb shot were set aside for use. Half were to be used in the Churchill and the other 50 were to be used on wheeled carriages. Since this was stated to be a priority job. Vauxhall set to work at once with their customary enthusiasm on the understanding that a production order would follow if trials were satisfactory. Design work (under the designation A22D) was completed by December 1941 and the pilot model, designated 'Carrier Churchill 3in Gun Mk I', underwent firing tests at Larkhill in February 1942. The 3in Gun Carrier was simply a Churchill chassis with a box-like armoured super-structure and front-mounted gun (plate 22). Considering its extemporised nature it was regarded as most successful on test.

However, the General Staff now changed their mind and reduced the provisional order for 50 gun carriers to 24. This was because the 6pdr gun was now available and they considered Churchill gun tanks with 6pdrs more important than the new and untried gun carrier which would use up valuable Churchill Chasis. Since Vauxhalls had ordered armour plate and parts for 50 gun carriers, however, they protested and got the original order reinstated. Shortly after, however, it was halved again. Newton Chambers undertook production, starting in July 1942. There was much delay, however, due to interdepartment bickering over its classification; was it a tank or was it self-propelled artillery? When it was finally classed as a tank the Department of Tank Design stepped in and requested many detail changes to make it acceptable to them, though since production had started no changes could be made. By late 1942 and early 1943 when production was complete, big progress had been made with the Challenger and no operational use could be seen for the Churchill 3in Gun Carrier. The few production vehicles therefore never fired a shot in anger, but some were converted to carry Snake equipment (plate 91) in 1943-44 but were used only for trials and training with this. The gun was removed in this conversion. Thus ended the short life of the only British tank with a really big gun in 1942, a promising design stifled by indecision.

The Black Prince

Ironically enough, a year after the demise of the 3in Gun Carrier the idea of mounting a high velocity gun in the Churchill was revived again. The original requirement of September 1941 envisage the use of the 17pdr gun in a turret even though a 3in gun in a limited traverse mount was subsequently used to overcome the problem of limited width and to speed up development. Long term studies for mounting the 17pdr gun continued, however, but were dropped late in 1942 when provisional plans were made to terminate Churchill production (see chapter 2). The Churchill remained in production, however, with a greatly improved version (the Mk VII appearing in November 1943. At this time Vauxhall were asked once more to go ahead with plans for a Churchill with 17pdr gun, this time using the new Mk VII as a basis for the design. This was to be regarded as an 'interim' design while plans were made for a new 'universal' chassis tank (which eventually emerged as the Centurion) by the Department of Tank Design.

Vauxhall's new design, the A43, was basically the Churchill VII with a wider hull to take a bigger turret mounting the 17pdr gun. For a time the A43 was known as the 'Super Churchill' but it was later officially named the Black Prince (plate 99). The original Churchill design had all along suffered from the limitation imposed on its overall width by the War Office which restricted all British tanks to British rail loading gauge dimensions. This in turn had a severe effect on turret ring diameter and so restricted armament size and development potential, a problem with all British tanks of the period before late 1943. Once this pre-war ruling was lifted (as it had to be if big guns were to be fitted) a new generation of tank designs became possible.

Work on the A43 started in January 1944 and prototypes were constructed by Vauxhall, their completion in May 1945 coinciding almost exactly with the first six Centurions. The Black Prince was similar in layout to the Churchill but a stronger suspension was fitted to support the heavier weight, and track width was increased to 24in. The Bedford Twin-Six engine and Merritt-Brown transmission were retained. Cupola was of all the all-round type as fitted in the Churchill VII, but it was shifted to the opposite side of the turret to clear the gun.

The vehicle weighed 50tons, had a crew of 5, 6in armour on the turret front, 5½in on the nose, 6in on the hull front and 3¾in on hull and turret sides. The 17pdr was the QF Mk4. The greatly increased weight with no increase in engine power reduced maximum road speed to only 10½mph with a much lower cross-country speed. Cessation of hostilities in Europe in May 1945 led to all work on the Black Prince being terminated, though troop trials were carried out on the six prototype models. Subsequently the A41 Centurion became the standard British tank of postwar years and the Black Prince remains only as an example of the ultimate development of the slow, heavily armoured infantry tank idea, a concept that was already virtually obsolete when the original Churchill was designed.

Though the Black Prince was arguably the best looking of the whole Churchill tank line and one of the best armoured and most powerfully armed British tanks of World War II it would undoubtedly have been something of a tactical liability had it seen service, due to its lack of power and poor performance.

6.
The Churchill Postwar

Churchills remained in service with the British Army for some twenty years postwar with Mk VII and Crocodiles of 7th RTR seeing service in the Korean War, 1950-52. The last production Churchill, a Mk VII left the Vauxhall factory in October 1945, by which time a grand total of 5,640 of all marks and variants had been built. No more basic models of the Churchill were produced after the Mk VII, but a completely new generation of special purpose variants was developed and produced by conversion from existing vehicles. By the mid1950s the Churchill Mk VII was completely supplanted by the Centurion and Conqueror as a gun tank but the new special purpose types were in turn playing an important part in supporting the fighting tanks. The new postwar variants are summarised here:

Churchill BARV: This was a Churchill Mk XI with turret removed and replaced with a large cylindrical superstructure over the turret ring to facilitate deep wading and consequent recovery of vehicles from beaches. Converted by the Royal Engineers it was a prototype only 1954-56. (plate 101). It proved unsatisfactory and the Centurion was subsequently adapted for the BARV role.

Churchill Twin Ark (FV 3901) (Linked Dog): developed from 1950, it entered service in 1954 to carry the heavy Conqueror tank over ditches and gaps. This device consisted of two Arks which could be linked together side-by-side, the two units forming a complete bridge. The Twin Arks were interchangeable and could be used on the left or right of the assault bridge, each unit providing one trackway of the bridge. As the Arks approached the gap to be bridged, they linked themselves together by coupling gear. The trackway of the Twin Ark was 7ft wide and consisted of a central fixed portion supported by four box sections welded externally to the hull. A folding ramp was attached by hinge at each end of the centre portion, and was folded on its deck when travelling. The ramps were opened by means of a system of steel wire ropes and pulleys coupled to a launching winch which was driven from the main engine. When opened and launched the ramps dropped freely to the ground. The Twin Ark was built on old Churchill III and IV chassis, and it must be stressed that this was an entirely different design from the original Churchill Ark. The term 'twin' referred to the folding ramps which were in two sections, and the fact that two vehicles could be coupled together. The Twin Ark could also be used singly to form a bridge for 'B' vehicles or light tracked vehicles (plates 121-123). This equipment remained in service until 1965 when withdrawal of the Conqueror and the introduction of the Centurion Ark rendered it obsolete.

Churchill Flail (FV 3902): this vehicle was a modified Churchill Mk VII fitted with a flailing device designed to clear lanes through enemy minefields by digging out or exploding the mines, and was a postwar design to improve on the wartime flails (Sherman, Crab, etc). The flail device consisted of a rotor drum fitted with 60 chains forming the flails, carried in front of the vehicle on arms pivoted on the hull sides and driven by an engine housed inside the hull in what had been the fighting compartment. A castor roller was provided on each arm and these served to keep the rotor at a constant height above the ground during flailing. When travelling, the whole flailing assembly could be hinged back on the roof of the vehicle. It was lowered into the flailing position with the aid of two other tanks. A fixed superstructure was built on top of the hull to replace the turret and was divided by a bulkhead to provide a driving compartment at the front and the flail engine compartment at the rear. The front of the structure was of thick armour plate and extended down to the lower front hull plate to protect the crew from debris thrown up by the flail and exploding mines. Lighter armour was used for the sides and the rear, and roof plate. Periscopes were fitted for the driver of the vehicle, and a vision cupola for the commander in what was previously the bow machine gunner's position. There were access doors to both compartments fitted into the roof plates. On the rear of the vehicle was mounted a Whyman Lane Marker assembly. The device fired markers into the ground every 40ft and could be set to fire on both sides or either side of the tank and was operated from the crew compartment. It was used to indicate a swept path for following vehicles. Weight of the Churchill Flail was 56tons and it had a crew of 2. This vehicle was sometimes (unofficially) known as the Toad (plates 119 and 120). Churchill Flails saw little service, most being kept in reserve for emergencies. They were discarded in 1965. Experiments were also carried out on a gutted Churchill Mk VII with flail equipment using radio control, but this did not proceed beyond the trials stage.

AVRE Mk VII (FV 3903): a postwar version of the wartime AVRE, this was the standard Churchill Mk VII fitted with a modified turret mounting a 165mm (6.5in) Ordnance BL Mk I low velocity gun, to replace the obsolete Petard type. The fully-rotating power-operated turret also mounted 12 smoke discharger cups fitted to the turret sides. Gunnery control was the same as in a gun tank. 31 rounds were carried. The AVRE Mk VII was developed from 1949 (plate 102) and entered service in 1954, supplanting earler AVRE models of World War II vintage (plates 103 and 104). It could be fitted with the Transportable Derrick *(qv)* plus the specially designed equipment detailed below.

AVRE Mk VII Dozer-Blade: the Churchill AVRE Dozer-Blade Equipment consisted of a hydraulically operated dozer blade, 11ft 5in wide and 3ft 2in deep with the necessary parts to convert the AVRE for bulldozing. Positioning of the blade was controlled from inside the driving compartment permitting close-support dozing tasks to be carried out while the crew were under protection of heavy armour. The equipment was also fitted to some Petard-armed AVREs in postwar years (plate 103).

AVRE Mk VII Fascine Cradle: for the purpose of carrying fascines (brushwood bundles) for use in the crossing of ditches and wide trenchworks, a collapsible steel fascine cradle was fitted on the front of the vehicle. The fascine cradle could hold a fascine 8ft in diameter, 13ft long and up to 10tons in weight (plate 105).

Churchill AVRE Mk VII (30ft Tank Bridge No 3): this device was a postwar (1949) version of the wartime AVRE SBG and consisted of the double tracked single-span No 3 Bridge, as carried on the Churchill Bridgelayer. In the launching position the front end of the bridge was attached to a frame on the front of the AVRE while the far end was supported by a wire rope passing over a derrick pole to a winch on the rear of the vehicle. The launching controls were operated from inside the vehicle. When travelling, the bridge was towed behind the AVRE on a two-wheeled trolley, being transferred to the launching position when the site was reached. Though intended for the postwar AVRE Mk VII, this bridge was also used in conjunction with the original Churchill AVREs which remained in postwar service. This arrangement was not altogether satisfactory, the weight of the No. 3 Bridge being too much for the suspension for sustained cross-country movement − hence the need for towing (plate 104).

Churchill APC (FV 3904): this was a postwar expedient to provide an armoured personnel carrier using an adapted Churchill Mk VII. The turret was removed and interior fitted out to transport a section of infantry with full equipment. Wireless equipment was installed and the hull machine gun retained. The few vehicles so converted appear to have been used only by the School of Infantry (plate 100). Some turretless Churchills of earlier marks had been used in 1944-45 as troop carriers, but these were local conversions.

By the mid 1950s development work was in hand on special purpose versions of the Centurion, and the Churchill's days were numbered. The Churchill Bridgelayer was replaced in about 1961 by the Centurion Bridgelayer and all other variants were officially declared obsolete in 1965 and any remaining were scrapped or expended as targets. The very last Churchills in the British Army were the AVRE Mk VIIs of 26 Armoured Sqn, RE, whose vehicles were replaced by new Centurion AVREs at a farewell parade at Hohne, Germany, in April 1965. The Churchill tank had come to the end of the road in the British Army after almost 25 years of arduous service during which time it had fought in all the major campaigns, been threatened with extinction (in 1942), had found a new lease of life in special purpose roles, and had ended up much respected to fade away like the traditional 'old soldier'. At the time of writing it still has not completely faded away, for a few Churchills survive (1969) with the Irish Army (plate 38). A few others remain with the Indian Army and one or two may survive with the Royal Jordanian Army.

A fitting tribute to the Churchill was made by Major-General G.L..Verney who, in a letter to *The Times*, wrote: 'I, and others who had the good fortune to fight in Churchill tanks will always maintain that the Churchill was the best all-round tank this side of the Iron Curtain'. It was certainly the most durable.

7.
The Churchill: an Illustrated Record

▲ 3

▲ 4

1. The original A20 project drawing for the 'shelled area' tank. The final disposition of armament agreed in the design stage is shown with 2pdr guns in the A12-type (Matilda) turret and hull front and a machine gun recessed into each side of the hull. **2.** The A20E1 prototype after arrival at Vauxhall's works where it is seen with a simulated wooden turret added for running trials. **3.** The A22 prototype running trials on the Vauxhall test ground. Similarity with the A20 will be noted though the hull is shorter and differs considerably in detail. Note the side air intakes and side escape door. **4, 5.** Two views of an early production Churchill I photographed on 9 May 1941 at Luton by the Vauxhall official photographer. Note the 3in. gun, lack of track covers, and exposed front horns, all characteristics of the early production vehicles.

▲6

▲7

▲8

▲ 9

6. King George VI inspecting the first production Mk I Churchill during a visit to the Vauxhall works in March 1941. first production Mk I Churchill during a visit to the Vauxhall works in March 1941. This vehicle has a mild steel turret though the hull is thought to be fully armoured. A few mild steel pre-production vehicles were built before T30971 shown here. **7.** An early examination of the tank which bore his name was made by Winston S. Churchill, The British Prime Minister. Here he rides in the second production Churchill I (right) and talks by radio-telephone to General Sir John Dill, C-in-C Home Forces, in the first production vehicle (left). **8.** In the Churchill II the bow 3in gun was eliminated in favour of a Besa machine gun. An early modification to all Churchills was the addition of dust plates inside the front horns (with suitable hull supports) to stop dirt and mud being thrown over the driver's and bow gunner's position and obscuring vision. This vehicle, on a training exercise in October 1942, is so fitted. **9.** An excellent view of a Churchill II with modifications described above. The triangular support plates can be clearly seen. Note also the rear dustguards and the distinctive asymmetrical shape of the cast turret. The case on the turret side (left) is for signal flags.

▲ 10

▲ 11

▲ 12

▲ 13

10. A 're-worked' Churchill II of a Canadian armoured· regiment seen during rehearsals for the Dieppe landing when the problems of disembarking from landing craft were investigated. This vehicle has the added track covers, though the side intakes have been removed in this instance to reduce the vehicle's width. 11. A comparative rarity was the Churchill IICS of which only one or two were built. This had the 2pdr gun in the hull and 3in howitzer in the turret. 12. An early production Churchill Mk II soon after delivery to a Canadian regiment in 1941. 13. The very earliest Churchill IIIs had the new welded turret and 6pdr gun on a hull which was built to Mk II production standards. Shown here is the first Mk III delivered to 56th Training Regt. RAC, at

Catterick in mid 1942 with instructors from the regiment giving it a trial run. 14. A top view of a Churchill II showing the external rear fuel tank in place.

▲ 14

▲ 15

▲ 16

▲ 17

▲18

▲19

15, 16. Two views of a Churchill III to full production standards with 6pdr Mk 3 gun, new air intakes with openings in the top, fully covered tracks and armoured covers over the exhaust pipe. **17.** The Churchill IV was identical to the Mk III except that it had a cast (instead of a welded) turret offering slightly better armour protection. It was built concurrently with the Mk III. **18.** First combat in which the Churchill took part was the Dieppe landing of 19 August 1942.

Here Mk IIIs of the Calgary Regiment are seen knocked out on the beaches after this largely abortive raid. Extreme right is one of the Churchill Oke flamethrower vehicles. **19.** The Dieppe raid gave the Germans an early chance to evaluate the Churchill. Here a German crew are seen testing a captured vehicle a week or two after the landing. This is a Mk III with track covers removed.

▲ 20

▲ 21

20, 21. The Germans also captured the earliest version of the Churchill flame-thrower, known as the OKE, at Dieppe, where three were landed to obtain operational experience with this type of vehicle. All were knocked out and captured, and these pictures come from a German Intelligence Report issued after the raid. Note the fuel reservoir at the rear with the flame pipe led forward above the track to the front horn. **22.** A view of the Churchill 3in Gun Carrier Mk I, an early experiment with the SP gun idea which never saw operational service though limited production was carried out. **23.** Three Churchill IIIs were used at Alamein, mainly to test them under

▲ 22

▲ 23

desert combat conditions. They played little part in the fighting but were the subject of numerous 'propaganda' pictures. Here all three are seen in typical Alamein dusty terrain. **24.** Another picture taken at Alamein shows a closer view of one of the three Churchills taking part. The canvas 'dodger' suspended across the front horns was to reduce dust thrown up to obscure the driver's and commander's view ahead.

▲ 24

▲ 25

▲ 26

▲ 27

▲ 28

▲ 29

25. Like other tank types used in the Western Desert, the Churchill was fitted with a canvas camouflage 'truck' body to disguise its shape against enemy reconnaisance missions. **26.** The Churchill finally vindicated itself in action in the Tunis fighting early in 1943. Here infantry follow under cover of a Mk III during the attack on Medje-el-Bab on 6 May 1943. The Churchill was more at home in the cover of the Tunis countryside than the Western Desert terrain. **27.** The Churchill IV (NA 75) was the first Churchill model to mount the 75mm gun. This was a North African (NA) local modification by Army workshops using American M3 guns and M34 mounts from damaged M4 Sherman tanks. Distinguished by the characteristic external mantlet, NA 75s remained in service (in Italy) until the war's end. Here five Churchill IV (NA 75)s line up with a Mk VII (third vehicle) to give concentrated counter fire on German gun batteries, Italian Front, April 1945. **28.** The service appearance of the Churchill was subject to numerous local modifications. Removal of all or part of the three-section detachable track covers was frequent as on this Mk IV. This vehicle, on the Italian front, also has covers added to its air intakes, presumably to combat the heavy rain of the period, winter 1944-5. Note the Mk 5 6pdr gun which was distinguished by its lighter appearance and counterweight. **29.** A typical Churchill III in service in Britain with full track covers fitted. Note the Bren gun on a bipod mount resting on the turret roof. In the distance is a Mk IV with Rotratrailer.

▲ 30

▲ 31

▲ 32

▲ 33

▲ 34

30. A closer view of the Churchill IV with Rotratrailer. This carried extra fuel and could be jettisoned when empty. It was rarely used in service, however, being too vulnerable. **31.** The Churchill V was a close support version of the Mk IV with a 95mm howitzer in place of the 6pdr gun. **32, 33, 34.** The Churchill VII (A22F) was a major redesign with integral instead of composite armour construction and with a new heavy cast/welded turret and 75mm gun. Features visible in these views include the circular (instead of square) side escape door, the vision cupola for the commander, vane sight, infantry telephone (at rear), armoured exhaust pipes and modified side detail. Note the intakes unshipped for transportation.

▲ 35

▲ 36

35, 36. Churchill VI was the Mk IV brought up as near as possible to Mk VII standards with vane sight and 75mm gun as an interim type before the Mk VII was available in quantity. **37.** By contrast the Churchill Mk X LT was a complete re-work to Mk VII suspension and gearbox, and a vision cupola as fitted in the Mk VII. This was a 1945 modification. **38.** Another view of a Mk X LT, this time used by the Irish Army post-was with more extensive appliqué armour added. **39.** The Churchill VIII was the close support version of the Mk VII with a 85mm howitzer in place of the 75mm gun.

▲ 37

▲ 38

▲ 39

▲ 40

▲ 41

▲ 42

40. The Churchill Crocodile was one of the best known flame-throwing tanks of World War II and carried its flame fuel in an armoured jettisonable trailer. Flame projector replaced the hull machine-gun and the tank could still use its main armament. **41.** A Churchill Crocodile demonstrates its capabilities on test. The armoured pipe for the flame fuel which passed under the belly of the tank is just visible by the 'link' attaching the trailer to the vehicle. **42,43.** The Churchill AVRE, based on a Mk III or Mk IV, was fitted with a Petard spigot mortar for demolition fire by assault engineers. Full conversion also included fittings on the side of the hull for CIRD and other equipment, visible in both these views. Plate 42 shows an AVRE in post-war service while plate 43 shows a heavily laden AVRE at Normandy in 1944 where the type was first used. The vehicle could carry a brushwood fascine on a wooden cradle as shown. Note the extra track shoes on the turret and hull for added protection. **44.** Another view of an AVRE in 1946 showing the normal arrangement for carrying the fascine. The retaining ropes were slipped from inside the cupola by way of a slip line (partly obscured

▲ 43

here) and the turret was traversed aft (or to the side) to give room for the facine. Retaining ropes, visible here, prevented the wood cradle slipping off the nose when the fascine was released. The vehicle shown is modified to Mk X LT standards with appliqué armour on hull sides, a vision cupola, and smoke dischargers. This vehicle also lacks CIRD fittings.

▲ 44

▲45

▲ 46

45. To enable commanders to see ahead when a fascine was carried on the AVRE, a periscope was developed for fitting to the vehicle's cupola. Shown here on a test vehicle at FVRDE, this device was not adopted. 46, 47. The Petard mortar was designed to fit on the 6pdr mount which greatly facilitated conversion to AVREs from existing Mk III and Mk IV Churchills. The co-axial machine-gun was retained and can be seen here both fitted and removed (as it was on some vehicles). The spring was to facilitate 'breaking' the barrel for loading. 48. The method of loading is seen here: the Petard barrel was 'broken' just outboard of the mount and loaded vertically through a sliding hatch which replaced the co-driver's access hatches. The projectile itself was called the 'Flying Dustbin' — for obvious reasons.

▲ 47

▲ 48

68

▲ 49

▲ 50

▲51

▲52

49. A post-war modification was the adoption of a properly fabricated steel (instead of wood) fascine cradle, and the use of a lighter but stronger Dumbell Fascine utilising steel 'Christchurch Cribs' developed by MEXE. The vehicle is an AVRE to Mk X LT standards, complete with vision cupola. **50.** All Churchill AVREs were fitted to carry the SBG (Standard Box Girder) bridge, which was topped up on sheerlegs and transported into position for release at the chosen site. The bridge could thus be placed under fire. A winch was fitted on the rear hull in a suitable carrier frame to enable the bridge to be hoisted into position on the vehicle. Purchase could be released by a slip rope from the turret. This AVRE with SBG bridge is seen at Normandy in June 1944 where this equipment was first used in combat. **51, 52.** Ardeer Aggie was an attempt to produce a more powerful AVRE weapon based on the Churchill. Recoil was neutralised in the Ardeer projector by firing a dummy projectile to the rear at the moment of firing the main projectile. The rear view shows the tube for dummy projectile in turret rear.

▲ 53

▲ 54

▲ 55

▲ 56

53. The Churchill ARV Mk I was converted from old Mk I gun tanks. Rear view shows all fittings of the vehicle including the portable jib seen erected on the nose. A Ram ARV Mk I stands in background. 54. The Churchill BARV was an experimental adaptation of the ARV Mk I with shingle plates added to avoid jamming the suspension.

55, 56. The Churchill ARV Mk II was a more completely equipped conversion based on the Mk IV chassis. These views show it with the 7½ ton front jib both rigged and stowed (note lower hull side stowage position). Used for many years post-war, some had a dummy 75mm gun (instead of a dummy 6pdr.

▲57

▲58

57. The Moyens Fascine Launcher was a device fitting to the turret instead of the hull and traversed by the turret. Shown here under test with a Dumbell Fascine, it was not adopted. 58. The earliest of the standard mat devices used with the Churchill was the TLC Laying Device and Carpet. Note how the arms attached to the standard AVRE CIRD fittings. 59. Twin Bobbins were carried on the same arms as the TLC Laying Device and provided a stronger trackway more suitable for armoured vehicles. 60. The TLC Laying Device and Carpet (Fascine Type) was a simple device mainly intended to provide a trackway for wheeled vehicles. It was soon superseded by the more sophisti-

▲ 59

▲ 60

cated carpet laying equipment. **61.** A Bobbin Mk I shown under test on Brancaster beach, Norfolk during pre-Overlord trials. Vehicle can be seen fitted with deep wading trunking on intakes and exhaust. Note the rigid frame.

▼ 61

▲62

▲ 63

62. The Bobbin Mk II, also seen at Brancaster, had a movable frame but a shorter length of carpet. **63.** Plough A (OAC Mk I) shown under test on an unarmed AVRE. Note the counter-weight frame at rear. **64.** The Plough B (Bullshorn Mk II), tested concurrently with Plough A, was a more compact and practical design. **65.** The

▲64

▲65

Plough D used the standard AVRE Atherton jib crane to raise it for travelling and to control the plough depth. It was tested with Ploughs A to C.

▲66

▲ 67

66. The OAC Mk II or Plough C under test. **67.** A more primitive device for lifting mines, tested concurrently with the ploughs, was an ordinary farm harrow towed behind a Churchill AVRE. **68.** The Bullshorn Mk IIIC Plough was one of the few equipments of this type actually used in combat during the invasion of France in 1944. It is here seen carried on a Churchill IV. **69.** The Jeffries Plough, here seen on an unarmed AVRE, was a simpler equipment similar to the Bullshorn. **70.** The Farmer Front device was designed to use the same arms as AMRCR equipment. It is shown raised.

▲ 68

▲ 69

▲70

▲ 71

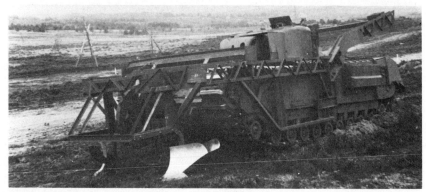

▲ 72

▲ 73

71. A similar but simpler device was the Farmer Track equipment which was distinguished by fewer tines and the 5ft diameter support wheels. **72, 73.** The Farmer Deck was a plough device carried on counterweighted frame. The close-up picture (73)

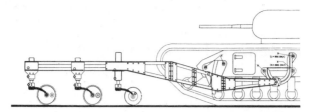

▲74

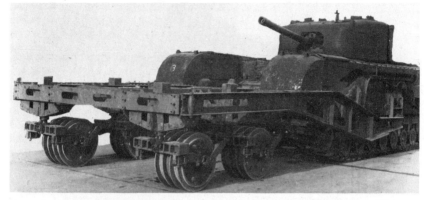

▲75

▲76

shows how it was carried for normal travelling. **74.** AMRA Mk IIe was the designation given to standard AMRA equipment ('Fowler Rollers') developed for fitting to the Churchill tank. **75.** The AMRCR was an improved development based on the AMRA device and utilising a similar carrier frame. **76.** A tight fit; trials with the AMRCR in 1943 included disembarkation tests from LCTs. A Churchill AVRE with SBG bridge is visible in the background.

▲ 77

▲ 78

▲ 79

▲ 80

▲ 81

77. The prototype 16in CIRD fitted to a Churchill AVRE. **78.** A production CIRD 18in with modified strengthened side arms. **79.** Another view of the 18in CIRD, this time to show the locating springs on the cross-bar. **80.** The experimental 21in CIRD, proposed as a replacement for the 18in model but never placed in production. **81.** The Light Carrot was one of the earliest explosive devices developed for carriage and positioning by a tank. It was ready in time for the Dieppe raid but does not appear to have been used in this action.

▲ 82

▲ 83

▲ 84

▲ 85

82. The Jones Onion was another early explosive device developed for use with the Churchill. The framework was supported from standard TLC mat layer type arms. 83. The Single Onion was a simpler version Device was similar to the Onion but was with a smaller quantity of explosive, shown here on a Churchill I. 84. The Quinson arranged so that the explosive charge could be hung over an obstacle (eg, a sea wall), rather than placed against it. 85. A prototype Goat under test showing how the explosive charge on its carrier platform was placed against the obstacle to be breached, in this a sea wall.

▲ 86

▲ 87

Also developed for use on the Onion frame equipment was a Bangalore Torpedo device in which two lengths of Snake explosive piping were carried vertically and released to fall over barbed wire and other light obstructions. The Bangalores were fired electrically via wire leads (visible here) attached to the bottom of the pipes. **89, 90.** The Snake device consisted of 20ft lengths of 3in water pipe fitted with explosives, and carried to the edge of a minefield where they were assembled into one long explosive pipe. The Snake was then detonated to explode any mines in the vicinity. This device was used operationally in 1944-5.

▲88

86. The Goat Mk III was the production version of the Goat and 400 of these were built though, so far as is known, they were never used operationally. **87.** The Elevatable Goat enabled the Goat charge to be placed against or over very high obstacles. **88.**

▲89

▲90

▲ 91

▲ 92

▲ 93

91. The old Churchill Gun Carrier was also converted to carry Snake equipment. It could carry 25 lengths of pipe instead of 16 as on the converted Churchill gun tanks shown in plates 89-90. This was an experimental conversion only. **92.** The Churchill AVRE with Conger 2in Mk I utilised an engineless Carrier as a trailer for the rocket and hosepipe which formed the basis of this mine exploding equipment. **93.** The Giant Viper was a postwar development from the Conger for use with the Churchill AVRE in which a specially designed trailer was used instead of a Universal Carrier. The

▲ 94

▲ 95

Giant Viper remained in use when the Churchill AVRE was replaced by the Centurion AVRE in 1965. **94.** The Atherton Jack was a portable jib crane which could be mounted on the Churchill turret to facilitate engine removal by means of a chain purchase as seen on this Mk I. **95.** The transportable derrick was used in conjunction with the Churchill AVRE as a kit to provide lifting capacity for engineering work in the field. Note the portable power plant mounted on the vehicle's rear and the wheels on the derrick for towing.

96. Whyman Mechanical Lane Marking Device seen fitted on a Churchill AVRE and showing flag pickets ready for firing into the ground. **97.** Assault sledges were another experimental project in which four armoured steel sledges were to be hauled behind a Churchill tank to carry infantry forward with immunity under fire. Tested in 1944, the idea proved impractical and was dropped. **98.** The Churchill II converted experimentally by Vauxhall with improved mechanical parts and rubber tyred road wheels in an attempt to improve performance. The rubber tyres led to its nickname of Pussyfoot. **99.** The Black Prince was the final development of the basic Churchill design. This view shows the wider hull and turret, the 17pdr gun, and the re-positioned air intakes. **100.** The Churchill VII APC (FV 3904) was a post-war conversion for the infantry carrier role. Note the footsteps for disembarking troops and the armoured shield forward of the turret ring aperture.

▲ 96

▲ 97

▲ 98

▲ 99

▲ 100

▲ 101

▲ 102

▲ 103

▲ 104

▲ 105

101. The prototype Churchill BARV of 1954 vintage **102.** The prototype of the Churchill AVRE Mk VII which was a 1949 design with a 165mm demolition gun replacing the Petard mortar used in the earlier AVREs. Production vehicles came into service in 1952-3. **103.** The production version of the Churchill AVRE Mk VII (FV 3903) had fittings to take a dozer (as fitted here), a fascine cradle, CIRD equipment and a No 3 Tank Bridge. **104.** Until well into the 1950s the earlier AVRE remained in service until supplanted by the new Mk VII model (plate 105). Like the AVRE Mk VII, the earlier AVRE was adapted to take the No 3 Tank Bridge. **105.** The Churchill Mk VII AVRE had a steel fascine cradle bolted to the nose. Note the release gear with slip line just above the turret.

▲106

▲107

106. The Churchill ARK Mk I had simple wooden trackways and short ramps, and was initially conceived mainly for enabling tanks to surmount a sea wall. **107.** The ARK I was also used to assist tanks to cross anti-tank ditches and other obstacles, and this view shows its mode of operation. **108.** The ARK II (UK Pattern) was distinguished from the ARK I by its longer ramps and kingposts.

109. The Churchill ARK II (Italian Pattern) remained in service post-war until the new Churchill Twin Ark replaced it. The vehicle shown is at Bovington in the early fifties. **110.** The Churchill Lakeman ARK seen under test in 1944 demonstrating its mode of operation with a Churchill IV climbing over it on to a dummy sea wall. This vehicle was a prototype only.

93

▲ 108

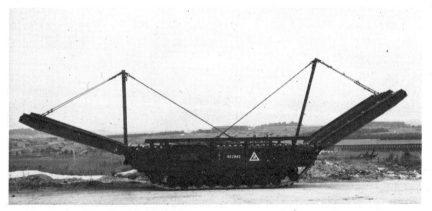

▲ 109

▲ 110

▲ 111

▲ 112

111. The Churchill Great Eastern Ramp shown from the rear with the rocket carrier and ramps in the travelling position. 112. The project model of The Churchill Hudnott ARK which was to be rocket operated. 113. The Churchill Woodlark was similar to the ARK but with higher trackways and rocket operated ramps. 114. The Churchill Bridgelayer with its bridge in the travelling position. 115. The Churchill Bridgelayer shown in service in Korea in 1951 emplacing its bridge across a ditch for the Centurions in the background to cross.

▲ 113

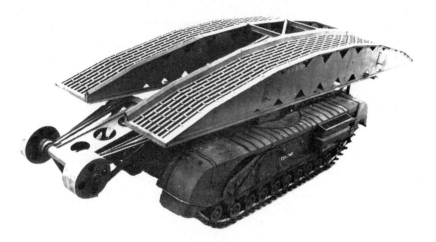

▲ 114

▲ 115

96

▲ 116

▲ 117

▲ 118

▲119

▲120

116. General Mark Clark, 5th Army Commander, with British staff officers, watches while a Mobile Bailey bridge is pushed into position over the River Senio in Italy in April 1945. 117. The Mobile Brown Bridge seen from the launching end with the turretless Churchill carrier vehicle second from the Churchill pusher tank far left. 118. The Mobile Dalton bridge was a refinement of the Brown bridge and this view gives a close-up of the carrier and pusher vehicles respectively. 119, 120. Front and rear views of the Churchill Flail, sometimes known as the Toad, with the rotor arms in the flailing position. For road running the rotor arms were lifted back hydraulically over the superstructure. Note the Whyman Lane Marker equipment at the rear in an armoured box.

▲ 122

▲ 123

121, 122, 123. The Churchill Twin Ark (Linked Dog) had double ramps launched and recovered by wire cables. While one vehicle could be used singly to provide a trackway for 'B' vehicles and light tracked vehicles, the Twin Ark was designed specially so that two vehicles could join together (Linked Dog) by the special lugs on the right hand of the trackway superstructure seen on the vehicle in plate 122. The linked vehicles then moved forward together into the gap to be spanned (plate 123) and launched their ramps. One commander controlled the linked vehicles by radio net. The Linked Dog provided a heavy duty trackway capable of taking the Conqueror and Centurion tanks. Churchill Twin Arks were in use from 1955-65 after which they were replaced by the Centurion Ark.

Appendix I:
Basic Specifications

The data tables opposite and overleaf give comparative details of the principal models of the Churchill. Some components remained virtually unchanged, however, as listed below.

Transmission: in all the various marks this was the Merritt-Brown regenerative steering system designed by Dr. Merritt, the Director of Tank Design, and built by David Brown Ltd. Mounted at the rear, this featured controlled differential steering combined with the gearbox and transmission. The first 115 Churchill I vehicles had 5 forward gears and reverse but later production variants all had 4 forward speeds. The Mark VII had an improved gearbox.

Suspension: independent suspension was used throughout with 11 bogies each side — all had triple helical springs except the last which only had a single spring. Bogie diameter was 13in.

Electrics: 12V main dynamo with an auxiliary petrol dynamo on the floor of the front compartment, and 2 x 6V batteries in series. The turret could be traversed by hand or by power.

Typical performance: trench-crossing, 6ft 9in; step, 4ft; fording (unprepared), 3ft; maximum gradient negotiable, 34°.

Elevation limits(gun tanks): 6pdr and 75mm, -12½° +20° ; 2pdr, -15° +20°

Tracks: three types of track were used: 1) heavy cast steel, 8.32in pitch with 70 links per track. Used on Mks I and II, and also on some of the early Mk III vehicles. 2) light cast steel, 7.96in pitch and 72 links, which was used on the later models. 3) manganese steel, 7.96in pitch and with 72 links, which was interchangeable with the second type, but was particularly used on the Mk VII and the Mk VIII. The distance centre-to-centre between the two tracks remained constant at 7ft 2½in, and the track width of 22in was unchanged throughout the series. Only the Black Prince had 24in tracks, the track width measurement being uncertain.

Wireless: the Number 19 set was used on all the variants, but a Number 38 set was also installed in the Churchill V, VI, VII and VIII; this unit was also fitted to the Black Prince.

Fuel: all variants carried 150 gallons, and Churchills I-VI also carried a 32½ gallon auxiliary tank. The radius of action varied between 90 and 125 miles.

Model	Engine Bhp/rpm	Speed (max) mph	Max Armour Thickness — Hull Front	Hull Side	Roof	Rear	Turret Front	Turret side	Turret Roof	Ordnance Designation	Production and/or Service period	Distinguishing features/remarks
Churchill I	Bedford Twin-Six (12 cyl) 325/2,200	17.3	89	76	15	50	101	89	29	Infantry Tank Mk IV, Churchill I (A22)	1941–42	Small cast turret and howitzer between front horns. Originally lacked track guards, added in "re-worked" vehicles.
Churchill II	"	"	"	"	"	"	"	"	"	Infantry Tank Mk IVA, Churchill II (A22A)	1941–42	As Mk I but without the front mounted 3in howitzer which was replaced by a 7.92mm Besa MG.
Churchill III	350/2,200	15.5	89* *101 with applique armour	76	19	50	88	76	19	Infantry Tank Mk IV Churchill III (A22B)	1942–43	Larger (welded) turret than previous marks, with 6pdr gun. Most had track guards as built and intake louvres with top openings. Very early vehicles had old pattern intakes.
Churchill IV	"	"	"	"	"	"	"	"	"	Infantry Tank, Churchill Mk IV (A22C)	1942–43	As Mk II (above) but with cast instead of welded turret. Vehicles converted to Churchill IV (NA 75) carried 72 rds of 75mm ammunition and had US 75mm M3 gun.
Churchill V	"	"	"	"	"	"	"	"	"	Infantry Tank, Churchill Mk V (A22C)	1943–44	Close support version of Churchill IV converted from Mk IVs by substitution of 95mm tank howitzer for 6 pdr.
Churchill VI	"	"	"	"	"	"	"	"	"	Infantry Tank, Churchill Mk VI (A22E)	Late 1943–44	Mk IV converted by substitution of 75mm gun for 6pdr.
Churchill VII	340/2,200	13.5	152	95	19	50	152	94	20	Infantry Tank, Churchill Mk VII (A22F)* *A42 from 1945	Late 1943–Late 1945	Major re-design with integral armour plate instead of composite construction. New heavy cast/welded composite construction turret and circular (instead of square) escape doors in hull sides. Modified hull side shape.
Churchill VIII	"	"	"	"	"	"	"	"	"	Infantry Tank, Churchill Mk VIII (A22F)	1944–45	Close support version of Churchill VII.
3in Gun Carrier	325/2,200	15.5	89	76	15	50	89	76	15	Carrier, Churchill, 3in Gun, Mk I (A22D)	1942	Box-like superstructure with 3in gun mounted low in the front. Limited production, not used operationally.
Black Prince	340/2,200	10.5	152	95	19	50	152	94	20	Infantry Tank, Black Prince. (A43)	1945	Widened and enlarged development of Churchill VII. Six trials vehicles only no production order.

Model	Crew	Battle Weight (Tons)	Length Overall ft	in	Height ft	in	Width Overall ft	in	Armament: Main	Secondary	Ammunition (rounds): Main	Secondary	Vision devices
Churchill I	5	38½	24 (ex track guards)	1.3/8	8 (ex aerial base)	2	10	8	1 x 2pdr 1 x 3in how.	1 x 7.92mm Besa MG 1 x 2in BT 1 x .303in Bren	150 x 2pdr 58 x 3in	4,725 x 7.92mm 25 x 2in Smoke 600 x .303in	6 periscopes 3 telescopes
Churchill II	"	"	"		"		"		1 x 2pdr	2 x 7.92mm Besa MG 1 x 2in BT 1 x .303in Bren	150 x 2pdr	6,975 x 7.92mm 25 x 2in Smoke 600 x .303in	"
Churchill III	"	39	25 (inc. track track guards)	2	8	2.9/16	"	"	1 x 6pdr Mk 3 or Mk 5	2 x 7.92mm Besa MG 1 x 2in BT 1 x .303in Bren	84 x 6pdr	6,975 x 7.92mm 30 x 2in Smoke 600 x .303in	5 periscopes 2 telescopes
Churchill IV	"	"	"		8	4.3/8	"	"	"	"	84 x 6pdr	6,925 x 7.92mm 30 x 2in Smoke 600 x .303in	"
Churchill V	"	"	"		"		"		1 x 95mm How Mk I	"	47 x 95mm	"	"
Churchill VI	"	"	"		"		"		1 x 75mm Mk 5	"	84 x 75mm	6,525 x 7.92mm 30 x 2in Smoke 600 x .303in	"
Churchill VII	"	40	24	2	8	10¾	10	10.3/8	1 x 75mm Mk 5 or 5a	"	"	"	7 periscopes 2 telescopes vision cupola
Churchill VIII	"	"	"		"		"		1 x 95mm How Mk I	"	60 x 95mm	"	"
3in Gun Carrier	4	39	25 (ex gun) 26 (with gun)	2 1	9	1	10	8	1 x 3in (20 cwt) Mk 3, 3ft, or 3* (Traverse: 5° each side elevation:-10° to +15°)	Nil	?	NIL	Vision flaps and 2 periscopes in cupola
Black Prince	5	50	28	11	9	0	11	3½	1 x 17pdr Mk 4	2 x 7.92mm Besa MG 1 x 2in BT	?	?	7 periscopes 2 telescopes Vision cupola

Appendix 2:
'Rework' Models and Projects

A summary of Churchill 'Rework' models and projects.

Mark	Characteristics and remarks.
Churchill IX	A Churchill III or IV retaining the 6pdr gun (Mark 3 or 5) but fitted with a new composite cast/welded A22F turret and extra *appliqué* armour.
Churchill LT	As above, but retaining the original turret modified by the addition of a vision cupola. Extra *appliqué* armour was sometimes added to the turret.
Churchill X	A Churchill VI((75mm gun) fitted with the new A22F turret and extra *appliqué* armour on the hull.
Churchill X LT	As above but retaining the original turret, modified by the addition of a vision cupola and vane sights.
Churchill XI	A Churchill V with the A22F turret s(a Mk VIII) and extra applique armour on the hull.
Churchill XI LT	As above but with the original turret, modified by the addition of a vision cupola and vane sights.
Churchill III*	A Churchill III with *appliqué* armour fitted as a field modification.
Churchill IV (NA 75)	A field conversion of a Churchill IV with a 75mm M3 gun fitted in place of the 6pdr. One Churchill III was similarly converted.
A21	A project for a lighter version of the A20. Abandoned at the paper stage in January 1941.
A23	A project for a lighter version of the Churchill to fulfill the Tank Board/Ministry of Supply requirement for a heavy cruiser tank. Never progressed past the paper stage, January 1941.
A26	A project calling for the revision of the A23 to meet a heavy cruiser tank specification. Paper stage only, January 1941.

Appendix 3:
WD Series Numbers

Since records of WD number allocation from 1942-45 are incomplete this listing is by no means exhaustive. It is compiled partly from such records as exist and partly from observation.

Number(s)	Vehicle	Builders	Remarks
T15124	Churchill I	Harland & Wolff	Mild steel pilot model
T15129	Churchill II	Vauxhall	Mild steel pilot model
T15130	Churchill II	Metro-Cammell	Mild steel early production (or pre-production) models
T15131	Churchill II	Birmingham Railway Carriage	
T30971-31420	Churchill I	Vauxhall	Production vehicles
T31421-31494	Churchill I	Dennis	Production vehicles
T31495	Churchill II	Dennis	Converted from Mk I
T31496-31655	Churchill II	Metro-Cammell	Production vehicles
T31656-70	Churchill III	Metro-Cammell	Production vehicles
T31575	Churchill II	Metro-Cammell	Converted to test vehicle for Petard mortar.
T31671-31745	Churchill II/III	Beyer-Peacock	Production vehicles
T31746-31820	Churchill III	Broom & Wade	Production vehicles
T31799	Churchill III	Broom & Wade	Used for experimental work
T31821-31995	Churchill III	Birmingham Railway Carriage	Production vehicles
T31997-32070	Churchill II/III	Newton Chambers	Production vehicles
S31997	Churchill 3 in Gun Carrier	Vauxhall	Prototype converted by Vauxhall from T31997
S31273-31321	Churchill 3 in Gun Carrier	Beyer-Peacock	
T32071-32143	Churchill I/II	Harland & Wolff	Production vehicles
T32071-7	Churchill I	Harland & Wolff	Production vehicles
T32078-32143	Churchill II/III	Harland & Wolff	Production vehicles
T32144	Churchill II (Pussyfoot)	Vauxhall	Experimental conversion
T32145	Churchill II	Vauxhall	Test vehicle
T32146-32245	Churchill II/III	Leyland	Production vehicles
T32246-32395	Churchill II/III	Leyland	T32246 in mild steel as Leyland pilot model
T32396	Churchill I	Gloucester Carriage	Mild steel pilot model
T32397-32470	Churchill I/II	Gloucester Carriage	Production vehicles
T65400	Churchill III	Leyland	Mild steel pilot model
T67867-67990	Churchill III	Birmingham Railway Carriage	Production vehicles

T67991-68140	Churchill IV	Metro-Cammell	Production vehicles
T68141-68315	Churchill III	Leyland	Production vehicles
T68316-68440	Churchill III (?)	Dennis	Production vehicles
T68441-68584	Churchill I/II/III	Broom & Wade	Production vehicles
T68585/68640	Churchill I/II/III	Dennis	Production vehicles
T68641-68715	Churchill I/II/III	Broom & Wade	Production vehicles
T68641-68715	Churchill I/II/III	Newton Chambers	Production vehicles
T68716-68840	Churchill III	Gloucester Carriage	Production vehicles
T68841-68918	Churchill IV	Beyer-Peacock	Production vehicles
T68919-68965	Churchill IV	Metro-Cammell	Production vehicles
T68966-69140	Churchill IV	Chas. Roberts	Production vehicles

NB: No record appears to have survived intact of WD numbers for later Churchill marks. The above allocations of block numbers were not necessarily fully taken up and the list does not take into account later conversions, etc. For instance Mk Vs and Mk VIs were converted from Mk IVs.

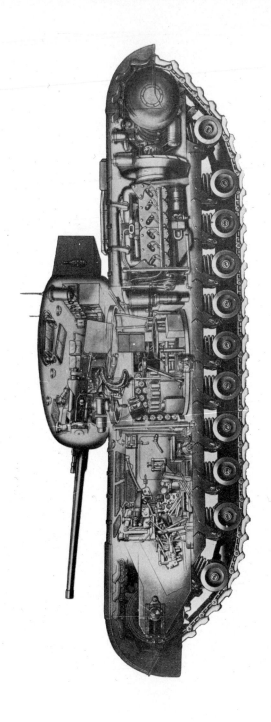

Appendix 4:
Churchill Fittings

Left; inside the Churchill; this 'ghosted' view of a Churchill IV clearly shows all salient features of the design. The four distinct compartments, from left to right, are the driving compartment, the fighting compartment (incorporating the turret basket), the engine compartment, and the transmission compartment. Features to note are the track tensioning screw in the front horns, front Besa machine gun and the driver's controls, the auxiliary generator motor behind the driver's seat, the ammunition stowage in the side panniers and in the turret basket, the hand traverse handle in the turret ring, and the No 19 wireless set in the turret rear. The roof-mounted bomb thrower is visible just above the breech of the 6 pdr gun. **Below;** an excellent view of an early Churchill Mk I under construction in 1941 shows the simplicity of the Churchill suspension with each bogie wheel pivoted from a bracket and compressed against a helical spring. The early form of intake louvre is also well shown.

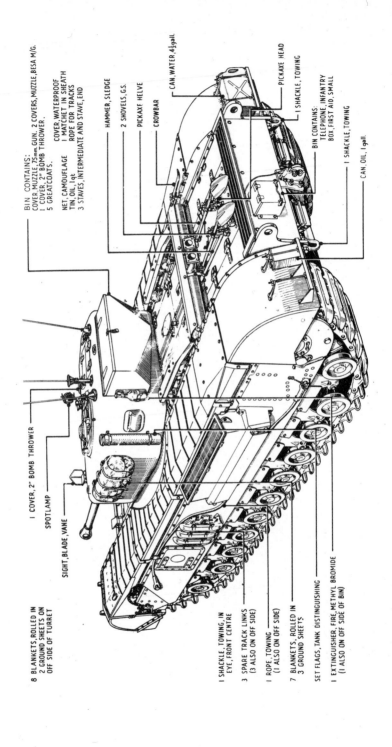

BIN CONTAINS:
COVER MUZZLE, 75mm. GUN, 2 COVERS, MUZZLE, BESA M/G.
1 COVER 2" BOMB THROWER.
5 GREATCOATS.

COVER, WATERPROOF

NET, CAMOUFLAGE   1 MATCHET IN SHEATH
TIN, OIL, 1 qt   ROPE FOR TRACKS
3 STAVES, INTERMEDIATE AND STAVE, END

HAMMER, SLEDGE

2 SHOVELS, G.S.

PICKAXE HELVE

CROWBAR

CAN, WATER, 4½gall.

PICKAXE HEAD

1 SHACKLE, TOWING

BIN CONTAINS:
TELEPHONE, INFANTRY
BOX, FIRST AID, SMALL

1 SHACKLE, TOWING

CAN, OIL, 1 gall.

1 COVER, 2" BOMB THROWER

SPOTLAMP

SIGHT, BLADE, VANE

8 BLANKETS, ROLLED IN
2 GROUND SHEETS ON
OFF SIDE OF TURRET

1 SHACKLE, TOWING, IN
EYE, FRONT CENTRE

3 SPARE TRACK LINKS
(3 ALSO ON OFF SIDE)

1 ROPE, TOWING
(1 ALSO ON OFF SIDE)

7 BLANKETS, ROLLED IN
3 GROUND SHEETS

SET FLAGS, TANK DISTINGUISHING

1 EXTINGUISHER, FIRE, METHYL BROMIDE
(1 ALSO ON OFF SIDE OF BIN)

Left; external stowage, Churchill Mk VI; typical for Mks IV-VIII. The infantry telephone at the rear allowed the commander to speak with personnel outside the vehicle under combat conditions. **Above;** top view of the Bedford Twin-Six engine and the rear-mounted Merritt-Brown gearbox shows how tightly the vehicle was designed to fit round this power unit. This engine is just about to be lifted out for maintenance. **Below:** for AA defence the Churchill was provided with a Bren gun, shown in close-up here on the two types of standard tank mounting which were normally stowed inside the vehicle. The weapon was used with 100 round drums or the standard magazine. Some Churchills had twin Vickers .303 "K" guns instead of the Bren and these were used on the standard PLM mount. The other mount (the Lakeman) was a simple stirrup type mount where an ammunition drum was necessary to clear the overhead arm.

Appendix 5:
Select Bibliography

The following publications include material relevant to the development history of the Churchill.

Liddell Hart, B.H.; **The Tanks: Volume 2.** Cassell, 1959.
Postan, M.M.; **British War Production.** HMSO and Longmans, 1952.
  – Hay, D. and Scott, J.D.; **Design and Development of Weapons.** HMSO and Longmans, 1964.
Select Committee; **Wartime Tank Production.** HMSO, 1945.
Vauxhall Motor Company; **Vauxhall: an account of our stewardship.** Vauxhall, 1945.

The following publications include detailed coverage of the operations, campaigns or actions in which the Churchill Tank participated. The list is not exhaustive.

Ellis, L.F.; **Victory in the West. Volume 1: The Battle of Normandy.** HMSO, 1962.
  Victory in the West. Volume 2: The Defeat of Germany. HMSO, 1969.
Liddell Hart, B.H.; **The Tanks: Volume 2.** Cassell, 1959.
Linklater, E.; **Our Men in Korea.** HMSO, 1952.
  Short History of the 51st Bn, Royal Tank Regiment. Privately published by the author.
McKee, A.; **Caen, Anvil of Victory.** Souvenir Press, 1964.
Robertson, T.; **Dieppe, the Shame and the Glory.** Hutchinson, 1963.
  History of **6th (Guards) Tank Brigade.**

Appendix 6:
Preserved Churchills

Churchill tanks preserved at the Royal Armoured Corps Tank Museum, Bovington, Dorset include a Churchill X LT, a Churchill VII (last production vehicle). a Churchill AVRE (Mk IV), a Churchill AVRE (Mk VII), a Churchill Twin Ark, a Churchill Bridgelayer, a Churchill Flail and the Black Prince. The RAC Tank Museum is open to the public daily (except at Christmas). Various other Churchill tanks are preserved and displayed at other military establishments but these are not generally on public view. A Churchill I is on display at the Canadian Armed Forces' Worthington Tank Museum at Camp Borden.